Guide to

PATIO AND HOUSEPLANTS

Guide to

PATIO AND HOUSEPLANTS

© Honos Verlag GmbH, Cologne
licensed special edition for
Naumann & Göbel Verlagsgesellschaft mbH, a subsidiary of
VEMAG Verlags- und Medien Aktiengesellschaft, Cologne
www.apollo-intermedia.de

Complete production:
Naumann & Göbel Verlagsgesellschaft mbH, Cologne
Printed in Germany
All rights reserved

ISBN 3-625-20756-7

Contents

Location:

sunny

semi-shady

bright

shady

Watering:

sparingly   normally

liberally

INTRODUCTION

In the living room or on a patio, plants instantly create a welcoming atmosphere. They improve the air quality in a room and they simply make people feel at home.

In this book, we will introduce you to the most important plant species for homes, balconies, patios and terraces. They represent a selection of the huge assortment available, with new species and types being added every year. It is wonderfully practical

that the great majority of houseplants can be moved to the balcony or terrace in the summer – and that this environment is actually very agreeable to them. However, you must not neglect to bring them indoors again in the autumn.

In the first part of this book you will find basic information about caring for your plants. The plant profiles that follow are arranged alphabetically according to their scientific names. The most common English names appear just below the scientific term. The profiles contain the most important characteristics and tips for caring for each plant. General rules which apply to all plants will not usually be repeated in the profiles.

The Question of Location

To ensure that a newly acquired plant will be comfortable in its new home and remain lovely to behold for a long while, make an effort to learn about the plant's needs ahead of time. The most critical factors are light and temperature, but humidity and air quality are also important. Most houseplants originate from tropical regions, and although the forms available today have been specially cultivated, they still prefer bright, light-filled and warm living spaces.

The move from a nursery – where plants grow under optimal conditions – to a windowsill is always a stress. Frequently, when moving into an apartment plants are forced to adjust to inferior light conditions, variable temperatures, dry, artificially heated air or draughts. For outdoor plants, both the regional climate and the plant's location are major factors in its well-being. Plants that have their origins in the tropics – such as bougainvillea – flourish best in warmer areas, whereas plants from maritime regions, like fuchsia, can also do well in cooler to temperate climates.

Light Conditions

A short detour into the basics of botany clarifies the importance of sufficient light. Plants have the ability to absorb carbon dioxide from the surrounding air and – with the help of their green colouring (i.e. chlorophyll), water and nutrients, and using the power of sunlight – convert it into carbohydrates, their actual source of nutrition. This process, called photosynthesis, simultaneously releases oxygen into the atmosphere. This explains why plants flourish in proportion to the light they receive.

Nevertheless, different plants do have different needs. Whereas plants that require a lot of light will not grow properly in a dark location – they will develop long, thin, soft shoots or bloom only weakly – shade-loving plants may wilt or literally burn up in a sunny spot, even if they are watered sufficiently. Plants with white or yellow variegated leaves require more light, since they contain less chlorophyll than green-leafed varieties. The same is true of red-leafed plants. In their case, the green chlorophyll has been replaced by another pigment. However, the amount of light a plant receives depends on more than the direction it faces. Curtains can significantly reduce light intensity, or trees and nearby buildings may cast shadows at certain times of day. Special Lux meters, available in shops, can measure the light intensity and show you where and when light is at its strongest.

Artificial light: In the darker months or in poorly lit corners, grow lights can be an enormous help for houseplants. Their spectrum contains a larger percentage of blue light rays, approximating the sun's light. It may be sufficient to simply move your plants closer to a window in the winter, or to transfer them to a south window.

On the shady side: Shade-loving plants can bring green to areas that are not blessed with so much light – such as north windows or north-facing balconies. In nature, they frequently grow under trees, and they are usually easy to care for.

Semi-shade: These plants are content with a few hours of morning or evening sun, and are most at home on the east or west side of the house.

Bright, without direct midday sun: Plants with an average need for sun will flourish best facing south-east or south-west, where they can enjoy the bright rays of the sun without being exposed to direct sunlight. Indoors, plants that need more light can be placed directly by a window, while those that tolerate more shade can be further inside a room.

The sunny south: Plants that need a great deal of light do best in direct sunlight – when indoors, on a sunny south windowsill. Flowering plants and species originating in southern climates, especially, feel most at home here. However, without the protection of a sun umbrella or Venetian blinds, these locations may be too hot for some plants at midday. They will lose too much moisture and begin to wilt. To prevent the heat from becoming trapped behind a windowpane, keep the window slightly open at this time of day or open the vents, if you have them.

When adding a new plant to a collection at a south window, it is best to keep it in a slightly shady place for the first 2 to 3 days. The same is true for plants that are moved to the balcony or terrace in the summer. They, too, need to adjust gradually to the greater light intensity of an outdoor location.

TIP

9

? If a plant is receiving too little light,

- it grows toward the light, produces long, thin shoots and only small, pale leaves and blooms very little
- coloured-leaf varieties and older leaves turn yellow
- the leaves dry out and fall off (particularly if the temperature is too high in the winter)
- only a few flowers are produced, and they wilt quickly (often in combination with high temperatures, insufficient humidity and/or nutrient deficiencies)
- the buds fall off (also caused by cold or lack of water)

! This helps:

Try a brighter spot or provide supplementary light. Adjust the temperature, water and nutrients according to season.

? If a plant is receiving too much light,

- the leaves of more sensitive plants will lose their colour or "burn" – that is, yellow or brown discolourations appear, which later dry out. The latter can also be a sign of excessive fertilising.
- cacti develop a reddish colour (especially in spring)
- the leaves wilt, even if the plant has been watered sufficiently (especially when heat becomes trapped behind a sunny windowpane)

! This helps:

Create shade or move the plant to a different location.

Temperature Requirements

In terms of temperature, summer provides good conditions for most patio and houseplants. Here again, the plant's native origins is key. However, when the days grow shorter and the season for artificial heating begins, problems arise for some houseplants. When temperatures are too high in relation to the available light, plants may react sensitively; insufficient humidity in heated rooms is an additional problem. Many plants prepare themselves for a rest period, when temperatures should be reduced along with the amount of available light. These plants should be moved to a cooler location, and watered and fertilised less frequently. Frost-sensitive container plants or houseplants that spend the summer outside need to be brought inside before the first frost. They should first be placed in a cool location before being moved into a heated living room.

Where to in winter?

During this season most house-plants prefer temperatures between 10–16 °C (50–61 °F). Still, many plants are content as long as temperatures are markedly lower at night. If they receive enough light, and the humidity is sufficiently high, they will survive the winter well in a cosy front room heated to 18–22 °C (64–72 °F). Others, however, prefer a cooler bedroom or hallway.

The soil temperature should be nearly as high as the surrounding air temperature. Even the most rugged species will not survive if it has "cold feet" and wet soil. Frost-sensitive container plants can spend the winter in bright, cool rooms, stairwells or winter gardens; some species can even be kept in dark cellars. As a general rule, the warmer the room, the more light is required, and the cooler a location is, the darker it can be. If plants are constantly kept in overly warm conditions, they become more susceptible to diseases and their strength is sapped. Specific instructions for wintering-over particular plants are given in the plant profiles.

If a plant is too cold,
- it stops growing and its leaves turn yellow
- the leaves hang down limply, especially when the plant's roots are too cold

This helps:
Increase the temperature or change the plant's location.

? ***If a plant is too warm,***
- the flowers wilt quickly or drop off; buds fall off prematurely (often in connection with low humidity and lack of light and/or nutrients)
- the plant may wilt or die
- the leaves turn yellow

! ***This helps:***
Reduce the temperature or change the location. In general, if the light intensity is high, plants can tolerate warmer temperatures. Keep in mind, however, that many species go through a rest period in the winter.

? ***If temperatures vary greatly or the location is draughty***
- the leaves turn yellow; they become deformed or fall off; the tips of the leaves turn brown
- the entire plant becomes sick

! ***This helps:***
Avoid draughts; be careful when airing rooms, especially when outside temperatures are below freezing. Seal any gaps or cracks in the windows. If necessary, move plants to another location.

Healthy Air

Fresh air, yes – draughts, no

Plants appreciate fresh air, but a plant in a draughty location will lose more moisture through its leaves than is good for it. Houseplants with thick, fleshy leaves, such as rubber trees or

kalanchoes, are less sensitive to this than more delicate varieties such as maidenhair ferns. When airing rooms, make sure your plants are not caught in a draught – or move them temporarily to a protected spot. Plants can also suffer cold damage in the winter, particularly if windows are not well sealed. Some houseplants cannot tolerate being directly above the rising heat from a radiator. The best plants for a windy outdoor spot are those that don't require much warmth. Plants also dry out quickly under these conditions, so species that need a lot of water are just as poorly suited to such locations as those with large, delicate leaves.

TIP

Just like people, many plants are highly sensitive to smoke – whether from an oven or from cigarettes – to fumes from paints or varnishes, or to gas or dust. This last source of damage is the simplest to remove: just wipe the plants regularly with a damp cloth, or mist them with a fine spray. If you plan to wallpaper or paint one or more rooms in your home, it is best to move your plants elsewhere. The thick-leafed species such as rubber trees or split-leaf philodendrons are relatively insensitive to "thick air". Other plants, such as spider plants or philodendrons, can even break down harmful substances. Nevertheless, the same rule applies: air your home regularly.

Humidity

Most houseplants originally come from warm, tropical regions where dew and rainfall keep the air naturally moist, and the relative humidity is around 90 per cent. In our homes, conditions are different. Air dries out as temperatures increase, and plants evaporate large amounts of water through the stomata in its leaves in order to "cool off". On hot days, many plants exert great effort transporting water from their roots to the upper regions of the plant. During the period when we heat our homes artificially, the relative humidity is often only 30 to 40 per cent. Only desert plants such as cacti and succulents can flourish at such low humidity levels. The majority of houseplants require an average relative humidity of 50 to 60 per cent. Plants native to tropical regions – such as orchids, bromeliads or some types of ferns – require much higher humidity as well as sufficiently warm soil. An enclosed plant window is the ideal location for these plants.

You can use a hygrometer to measure the humidity exactly.

TIP

Increasing the humidity

Mist leaves regularly to increase the humidity, on the underside as well as the upper surface. Use only room temperature, softened water or water that has been allowed to stand. This avoids subjecting the plant to a cold shock or producing unattractive spots from lime deposits. Flowers will also become discoloured easily, so try to protect them from the water stream. Do not mist plants that are standing in the midday sun; water drops will intensify the sun's effects and create burned spots. Allow enough time for the plant to dry off before evening comes.

Not all houseplants can tolerate being misted from top to bottom. Plants with soft, hairy or fuzzy leaves are one example. Such plants are more grateful if they are placed in a gravel-filled saucer filled with water. Alternatively, you can fill the space between the plant's pot and the planter with expanded clay and moisten the clay.

Vaporisers attached to your radiators, indoor fountains or electric humidifiers can also increase the humidity in your home and improve the overall atmosphere of the room.

 ### If the humidity is too low,
- the tips of the leaves turn brown, the leaves themselves become yellow and roll inward or wither;
- flowers wilt rapidly and buds fall off prematurely;
- infestations of spider mite are a frequent occurence, since these insects flourish in dry air.

 ### This helps:
Mist your plants regularly. Change the location if necessary. Choose less sensitive species with thick, leathery leaves.

? If the humidity is too high,

- small, yellowish-green spots appear on the leaves, which over a period of time turn brown and dry out. So-called "cork spots" can also be the result of irregular watering or a lack of light.

! This helps:

Heat and ventilate rooms sufficiently.

Special Locations

In bedrooms, the temperature is usually fairly constant and not overly warm. Cyclamen is very thankful for this type of location, as are plants which prefer cooler temperatures (ca. 15 °C/59 °F) in winter. However, some sensitive people are susceptible to headaches from strongly scented plant species.

In bathrooms, provided, of course they have a window. All plants that prefer warm temperatures and high humidity will grow well here. This is true of most ferns, but also peace lilies, dieffenbachia, cyperus, mind-your-own-business and many others.

Entryways and hallways are generally cool and not well lit. Here, you should choose hardy, easy-to-care-for specimens such as the yucca, philodendron or spider plant. No plant, however, will tolerate draughts on a regular basis.

17

Empty corners are a good place for large plants. Attractively coloured or unusually shaped plants can brighten up a dark area of the room, as well. One or more large plants can work well as a room divider.

Many houseplants come into their own if they are allowed to spend the summer months **out in the open**. Nevertheless, wait until after mid-May, or whenever the danger of frost is past, to place your plants outside. Even then, allow them to get used to the strong spring sun gradually. When placing houseplants outdoors, it is best to choose a location sheltered from wind.

Caring for Your Plants

Watering

Water dissolves and transports nutrients; when it evaporates, it cools the plant off. How frequently we need to reach for the watering can depends, first of all, on the specific needs of each plant, but also on the conditions unique to a location and on the plant's container. Since they have a larger surface area from which water can evaporate, plants with large, soft leaves require a great deal of water. Species with fleshy, leathery or small leaves evaporate less water, or may even be able to store it; thus, they are better equipped to survive dry periods. Smaller pots need to be watered more frequently than large ones; plastic containers hold moisture in longer than clay or terracotta pots. Sandy soils dry out faster than loamy ones.

The right way to do it:

- Check your plants' water needs daily ("finger test"). Even in rainy weather, it is possible that balcony plants will not receive enough water, since a large portion of the rainwater often runs off thick masses of leaves.
- It is best to water in the morning or evening. In order to avoid unsightly spotting on the leaves, never water in the direct midday sun or from above.
- Water less frequently, but allow the water to permeate the soil completely.
- Water cacti and succulents only when the soil is completely dry.
- Most species will not tolerate standing water.
- If a pot or a hanging basket becomes completely dried out, place the plant in a water bath and allow it to remain until no air bubbles rise to the surface.
- Azaleas and orchids, for example, require water that is low in lime. In this case, collecting soft rainwater is a good idea.

If plants are watered too much,

- the leaves turn brown, particularly at the edges, and may even fall off (usually in cases of standing water)
- the base of the stem will rot

This helps:

Allow the root ball to dry out; give that plant less water in the future. Make a finger test before watering – that is, feel the soil surface for moisture. For plants that rot easily, it is best to water via the saucer rather than from above. Be sure there are drainage holes at the bottom of each pot so that water does not remain trapped inside.

? If plants are watered too little,
· the leaves hang down limply, dry out and fall off.

! This helps:
Water the plant immediately; loosen the top layer of soil. If the root ball is very dry, immerse the plant in a water bath.

? If plants are watered irregularly,
· buds fall off prematurely; flowers do not mature.

! This helps:
Check the soil surface daily ("finger test") and water as soon as it becomes necessary.

Holiday periods

Surely you are familiar with this problem: who will care for your beloved plants while you are on holiday? If you are lucky, you can rely on friendly and helpful neighbours. If you cultivate your plants hydroponically, the solution is simple. When you plan to be gone for a long time, you can simply fill the container to its maximum volume.

Balcony boxes and hanging baskets are also available with water tanks that can keep your plants supplied with water for up to two weeks. If you move your plants to a shady spot before you leave, and cut off the blossoms, they will evaporate significantly less moisture. You can also place the plants in a saucer filled with water or a bowl filled with clay granules that have been completely saturated. This will reduce their need for water.

In smaller pots, you can employ a wicking or tapering system to supply the plants with water.

If you are technically inclined, you can even install an automatic irrigation system which turns its small hoses on with the help of a clock timer or a tensiometer (moisture gauge). The system can be connected directly to your water tap.

Fertilising

Supplying your plants with fundamental nutrients – including nitrogen, phosphorus, calcium, potassium and magnesium – and trace minerals, such as iron, is just as important as supplying them with water, since these nutrients are quickly exhausted within the confines of a container. If you give your plants an initial treatment with organic fertiliser or time-release fertiliser the nutrients will be released gradually. If necessary, you can supplement once a week with a quick-acting complete mineral fertiliser. If a plant is growing only weakly, its leaves turn yellow or even fall off, it is high time for a dose of fertiliser. In order to avoid overdosing or burning always follow the dosage instructions.

Symptoms of deficiency

Nitrogen (N): Nitrogen is a significant component of chlorophyll. If it is deficient, the older leaves will fade in colour and the plant's growth will slow noticeably.

Phosphorus (P): A phosphorus deficiency makes itself known through meagre flower development and slow growth; the leaf undersides and stems turn reddish in colour.

Calcium (Ca): If a plant receives too little calcium, its shoot tips, flowers and roots become deformed and fade in colour. The veins of the leaves turn brown, and the stalks may wilt.

Potassium (K): Potassium facilitates the absorption of water and development of supporting tissues. If potassium is lacking a plant wilts, the edges of the leaves fade in colour (chlorosis), and these areas eventually die off.

Magnesium (Mg): With a lack of magnesium, the areas between the leaf veins fade in colour – especially in older leaves, which then die and fall off.

Iron (Fe): If this mineral is missing the plant will display chlorotic symptoms like those seen in a magnesium deficiency; however, the leaf veins remain green.

The right fertiliser

Complete mineral fertilisers: Multi-nutrient fertilisers contain all the important basic nutrients and trace minerals and plants can absorb them quickly. They are available as liquid, powder or as fertiliser sticks, and are appropriate for supplying plants with nutrients quickly in the main growing period.

Time-release fertilisers (long-term fertilisers): These fertiliser pellets release nutrients little by little – over a period of three, six or nine months depending on the product. A plant treated with a time-release fertiliser will not need fertilising again for several weeks.

Special fertilisers: Single-nutrient or trace mineral fertilisers can be used selectively to balance out a deficiency in one or more nutrients – e. g. a special iron fertiliser. Plants such as azaleas, which are sensitive to lime, require a fertiliser which will not increase the acidity (pH value) of the substrate. Other fertilisers are may be tailored to the nutritional needs of certain species – for example, cactus fertiliser.

Organic fertilisers: These animal or plant-based materials are transformed gradually in the soil, so that they have a long-ranging effect. The disadvantage, however, is that they cannot regulate an acute deficiency quickly.

Plant tonics: These substances do not directly supply the plant with nutrients; rather, their physical and chemical properties encourage plant growth. Some examples of plant tonics are stone meals, valerian extracts or algae. Plant-based liquid manures – for example, from stinging nettles, dandelions or horsetail grass – simultaneously work as natural pesticides.

The right way to do it:

- Since plant roots are delicate, it is gentler to fertilise more frequently and in lower doses than to give high doses less often. This is particularly true for salt-sensitive plants. Furthermore, the soil does not require any more nutrients than the amount that the plant takes out, so be sure to follow dosage instructions carefully.
- Freshly re-potted plants do not need to be fertilised again for four to six weeks; during this time they will have developed sufficient new roots.
- If you treat a plant with a time-release fertiliser at the time of planting, you will not need to fertilise again for approximately ten weeks.
- Only fertilise when the substrate is sufficiently moist.

Soils and Substrates

The term "substrate" has a Latin origin and means something like "foundation". Particularly potted plants, whose nutrients are not replenished by the earth, require an optimal substrate. It should have the following characteristics:

- Primary and trace nutrients are present in sufficient and balanced amounts.
- The substrate has a loose and stable structure, meaning that it contains sufficient oxygen. This is particularly important for large plants, which will remain in the same pot for a long time.
- Water must be able to drain well so that no standing water builds up. On the other hand, the substrate should also be capable of storing enough water that the plant does not need to be watered constantly.
- A pH value of 5.5 to 6.5 is ideal for most patio and houseplants.
- It goes without saying that a plant substrate should be sterile.

Standard potting soil: This is of uniform quality and contains primarily white peat or a peat substitute, clay minerals and humus. The available products range from low-nutrient cultivation soil to soils containing time-release fertilisers. The pH value of 5.5 to 6.5 is optimal for the majority of houseplants.

Peat growth medium/Potting compost (TKS): TKS substrates consist primarily of limed white peat. This material is very loose, but also dries out quickly and does not absorb water well. TKS works well for loosening up heavy, loamy soil. In recent years, as moors have become increasingly scarce, white peat has frequently been replaced by substitutes like bark humus or coconut coir.

"Flower soil": The many types of soil available in shops vary widely with regards to quality. In low-priced substrates, a portion of the white peat is often replaced by black peat, a material which is heavy, poorly aerated and easily leads to standing water. It is well worth paying for higher-priced quality products, often labelled as "gardening quality".

Special soils: These substrates have been tailored to the specific nutritional needs of certain plants. Thanks to its high sand content, for example, cactus soil is very porous and low in nutrients. This is an appropriate soil for succulents. Palm soil contains a high proportion of clay or loam and also provides more stability for large plants. Orchid substrate has a very loose structure, usually consisting of a mixture of peat fibre, fern roots and moss. Rhododendron soil, with a pH value below 5, is extremely acidic and thus ideal for azaleas and other lime-sensitive plants.

"Homemade": Mix garden earth (which should be loamy and humus), well decayed compost, sand and white peat (or a peat substitute product) in proportions of 3:3:2:2. The disadvantage of this do-it-yourself mixture, however, is that its quality is usually not uniform and it is not as sterile as industrially produced substrates.

Hydroponics: Hydroponic substrate consists of burned clay granules – so-called expanded clay. A water level meter signals when it is time to add water to the pot, and you should always wait until the "minimum" water level has been reached. The advantage of hydroponics is much less frequent watering. In addition, the clay granules constantly evaporate water, increasing the humidity of the surrounding air. Since the granules do not retain any nutrients, it is necessary to fertilise approximately every three months with a special time-release fertiliser.

Not all plants are equally well suited to hydroponics. The plants that adjust best to this method are those with thick, strong roots. Only young, healthy plants can survive the change from soil to hydroponic culture. To ensure that the roots don't rot, it is essential to wash every last crumb of soil from the roots. Another consideration is the fact that hydroponic containers and granules are relatively expensive compared to soil cultivation.

Clay granules: Air-foamed chunks of clay are a good alternative to pure hydroponics. You can transfer a plant into the clay granules along with its soil ball; the clay granules function as a water reservoir. Here, too, a water level meter signals when the plant needs a fresh supply of water.

Re-potting

Since even the best substrate is eventually exhausted, regular re-potting ensures that your plants remain lush and healthy. Do not wait to re-pot until the plant is already growing poorly, has stopped blooming or the roots grow through the pot. Hard water and residues from mineral fertilisers can make a substrate overly salty. This is clearly evident when sediment becomes visible on the surface of the soil. Here, too, a fresh substrate will greatly benefit your plant. The same is true if moss has begun growing on the soil surface and roots begin rotting from standing water. Be sure to check any new acquisitions as well: they may be planted in pots that are too small.

The right way to do it:

- As a rule of thumb, re-pot mature plants every 2–3 years. Fast-growing specimens may require yearly re-potting.
- If it isn't possible to re-pot, at least exchange the top layer of substrate and supplement with a time-release fertiliser.
- Spring is the best time for re-potting, but avoid the blooming period whenever possible. Otherwise, the plant will grow more new shoots instead of flowers.
- Moisten the earth ball well before re-potting. This allows you to remove it from the pot more easily.
- Loosen the root ball once the plant is removed from the pot. To encourage rapid growth of new, fine roots, prune long roots slightly and remove any brown or rotted sections.
- Prune the roots if you want the plant to maintain its present size, keeping the root volume proportional to the size of the plant.
- For smaller plants, the new pot should be 2 cm (1 in) larger in diameter; for larger plants, 5–10 cm (2–4 in). Previously used pots should be cleaned thoroughly.

- Remember to include a drainage layer on the bottom of the container. This can consist of broken clay potshards or expanded clay granules.
- To prevent the stalk from rotting, the plant should stand at the same depth in its new pot. Press the earth ball firmly.
- Water the plant generously. In order to encourage rapid growth, however, keep the plant somewhat drier for the next two weeks. Place it in a bright location, but away from direct sunlight. Add fertiliser in approximately six weeks.

Clay or plastic pots?

Clay: Clay pots allow the substrate to aerate well, and water dries out relatively fast. These conditions are ideal for cacti and succulents; however, clay pots are less well suited to plants that require a lot of water. Clay pots are heavy and, unfortunately, breakable; on the other hand, their greater weight makes them more stable.

Plastic: Advantages are the pots' light weight and comparatively low price. Plastic pots allow water to evaporate very slowly, making them a good fit for moisture-loving species. The substrate heats up quickly.

TIP

All containers – of either clay or plastic – must have drainage holes at the bottom to prevent water from accumulating.

To Prune or Cut Back?

If you regularly cut or pinch off all **wilted** blossoms and leaves, plants will direct their energy to the formation of new flowers rather than going to seed. This allows you to enjoy your petunias, summer daisies, lady's slippers and other flowers much longer. After a brief rest period, the plants will go into full bloom again.

Many species will reward a good **pruning** with vigorous flowering. If you regularly thin out older container plants they will maintain an attractive shape and continue to bloom. Simply remove any dried out branches or long, thin shoots in the spring. The trim will be barely noticeable if you only cut back as far as the side branches.

A radical, **rejuvenating trim** is a good treatment for a plant that starts to look bare or has ceased to grow or produce flowers. Remove any weak shoots and cut all the other branches radically; older limbs can even be pruned directly above the ground or near to the trunk.

For plants that bloom continuously from spring through the end of summer, wait until the plant's rest period to prune. Then you can confidently give the plant a significant trim. More detailed pruning instructions are given in the plant profiles.

To cultivate high-stemmed plants, remove all the side shoots from the young plant initially, until the plant has reached the desired height. Then trim the top of the plant so that the side branches can develop. Continue pruning the side branches until the final crown has taken shape. Remove any shoots from around the trunk.

TIP

Propagating Your Own Patio and Houseplants

For many gardening enthusiasts, few pleasures are keener than that derived from cultivating their favourite plants themselves and watching them grow to maturity. Propagation via seeds, cuttings or other methods is not at all expensive and in most cases can be done at any time of year.

Whereas there sometimes can be variation between seedlings, asexual, vegetative propagation (e. g. via cuttings or division) has the advantage that you can quickly acquire one or more identical offspring of your favourite plant. These methods are appropriate for plants that require a long period of time from sowing to maturity, or for plants that are sterile – that is, they don't produce seeds. The best time for these methods is springtime or early summer. For propagation to succeed, however, you need to start with a strong and healthy parent plant. The containers and substrates required are the same as those used for raising seedlings.

Seedlings

The **best time period** for generative propagation – the technical term for sexual propagation via seeds – is in the spring and summer. During this time, the young plants can profit from the increasing supply of available light. When buying seed packets, be sure that the expiration date has not passed; otherwise, their capacity for germination will certainly be reduced. Always store seeds in a dry, well ventilated place and avoid exposing them to the sun for long periods of time.

TIP

You can harvest seeds from many plants yourself. Cut off the ripe seedpods, lay them in a bowl or box, and place them in a dry, well ventilated spot for several days. When the pods have dried out, shake out the seeds and save them in paper bags or screw-top jars until time to plant. The offspring from home-harvested seeds are usually not as uniform as those produced from commercial seeds, so be prepared for a few surprises.

Containers: Clay flowerpots, plastic trays or Styrofoam boxes are all fine containers for sowing seeds, provided they are clean. If you wish to work more professionally, you can purchase a propagating case with a transparent cover – or even a miniature greenhouse complete with a heater and temperature gauge or heated propagating dishes. If you use a multiple-pot panel, you can re-pot each young plant with a solid soil ball. Pressed peat pots that swell when watered have the same advantage.

Substrates: You can either buy special propagating and sowing soils or mix one yourself. To make your own, mix one part each of

regular potting soil, peat and sand. It is a good idea to heat the mixture in a very low oven for about 30 minutes in order to kill any germs. Propagating soils need to be loose, since seedling roots are extremely fine. If the soil is overly fertilised, the roots can easily "burn".

Procedure: First fill the propagating container with the cultivation soil and level off the surface. Sow the seeds loosely, press them down gently and water well with a fine stream of lukewarm water. You can also proceed the other way round – first watering the soil well and then sowing. If the seeds are very fine, it is best to mix them with sand so they will be distributed better. Dark-sprouting seeds should be covered with soil; light-germinating varieties should simply be pressed down gently. You should never allow the substrate to dry out, and since the seeds require constant high humidity you should cover the sown containers with transparent film, a plastic lid or similar cover. Newspaper can be used to protect the seedlings from burning in strong sunlight. Most species require temperatures of 18–20 °C (64–68 °F) to germinate; some exotic plants may require higher temperatures. As soon as the seedlings have developed roots, the cover should be removed.

Pricking out: When the propagating container becomes too crowded, it is time to separate the seedlings and prick them out into individual pots. A special soil for sowing and pricking out makes a good substrate, since it is only lightly fertilised. Be careful not to plant the seedlings any deeper than they were before. To ensure that the plants branch out well, simply trim off the main shoot as soon as the plant has at least three leaf stems.

Fern spores: The undersides of older fern fronds are often thickly covered with spores. You can simply knock them off and sprinkle them into a container, on a substrate of moist, part-peat soil. Cover the spores and place the container in a warm place, in a saucer filled with water.

Cuttings

Top cuttings: These soft, non-woody cuttings should be cut from one-year-old shoots that have not yet shown signs of blooming. Such cuttings root very easily. Cut the shoot just below a leaf node; it should be 5 to 10 cm (2–4 in) long and not have too many leaves. It is best to remove the lowest leaves. In large-leafed varieties, the leaf surface area should be reduced by half to reduce evaporation and accelerate root development. Stick the cuttings into the propagating soil, approximately 2 cm (1 in) deep, press gently

and water well. For species that root only with difficulty, a special rooting medium is recommended. Finally, cover the cuttings with transparent film or a lid and place them in a bright, warm location. Warm soil will encourage root development. It is important to air the containers occasionally. Cuttings from cacti and succulents should not be covered, since they can rot easily. As soon as the cutting develops new leaves, you can remove the cover entirely. When the new plant has grown enough roots it is ready for re-potting in a fresh substrate.

Section cuttings: Section cuttings, or pieces of shoots, should also be cut just below a leaf node. The advantage of this method is that you can obtain several cuttings from a single shoot. Otherwise, the procedure is the same as for top cuttings.

Stem or cane cuttings: Cut a strong, leafless stem into sections ca. 10 cm (4 in) long. These should be planted vertically, with the cut edge downward, 5 cm (2 in) deep in propagating soil.

TIP

Many cuttings will also root in a glass of water. Adding a piece of charcoal to the water will prevent the plant from rotting. You can re-pot the cutting as soon as it has developed enough roots.

Leaf cuttings: Some plants will produce new plants from cut-off leaves or sections of leaves. Place the leaf or leaf piece with the cut side down in fresh propagating soil and keep it uniformly moist. New plantlets will grow exactly at this spot. In the case of succulents, allow the leaves to rest for a few days before planting to allow the cut edge to dry out.

Additional Methods

Division: This method works well for plants with multiple shoots or those that produce rhizomes. This type of propagation can be conveniently combined with re-potting; the best time to do this is spring or early summer. Water the plant well before you begin. Often, the plants will separate by themselves when you loosen the root ball; otherwise, separate the ball with your hands or with a sharp knife. Place the separated parts in fresh substrate and let them continue growing in a bright location.

Bulblets: As soon as the leaves have died off – usually in the early summer – you can separate the small offsets from the parent bulb. They should be stored in a dry place until the autumn planting time.

Plantlets: Some plants, such as the kalanchoe or the piggyback plant, do our propagating work for us. Young plantlets, complete with roots, grow on the leaves of the parent plant. You can simply separate these offspring and plant them in pots.

Separating offshoots: These completely developed mini-plants – which are usually found at the base of the parent plant – can be separated along with their roots and re-potted immediately.

Runners: The parent plant develops long, horizontal stems, on the ends of which independent new plantlets grow – often complete with roots. You can simply cut them off and plant them in pots.

Layering: Hanging or climbing plants frequently develop roots at the nodes of their long shoots. At this point you can plant a shoot in a pot and wait until it produces roots, then simply separate the runner from the parent plant.

"Mossing": Make a wedge-shaped cut in the stem of a plant, below a leaf node, at the point where you wish a new root to grow. Place a solid object in the cut to keep it from growing back together. Then wrap moist moss and plastic film tightly around the area until new roots begin to develop. Finally, you can cut off this section of the stem and plant it in a pot.

Grafting: Grafting is the process of combining two plants by connecting the sprouting section of one plant with the lower section of another.

Cacti are usually easy to graft; the best time to do so is in spring or summer. Remove the upper section from the base plant using a sharp knife, and cut a groove in the base. Cut off the portion to be grafted, press it into the base plant and secure with a rubber band. Place the plant in a bright, well ventilated location and keep the soil slightly moist. It is very important not to touch the cut edges.

Hygiene is the greatest command-ment as far as all propagation work is concerned. In order to avoid infections, always be sure to use clean containers and sharp, sterile knives.

Seedling diseases: These are most often caused by *Pythium*- or *Phytophthora* fungi, which commonly attack young tissues or wounded areas. The fungi cause the upper roots and the base of the stem to turn brown; the roots rot, the young plants wilt and finally simply tip over. These fungi frequently occur when the plants' location is too moist. You can treat your plantlets pro-phylactically by watering them in the propagating bed with a seedling disease preventative that is available in shops. Any plants that have already been infected must be removed from the bed and destroyed.

Pests and Diseases

Prevention

You can get off to a good start by purchasing only healthy, strong and pest-free plants and providing them with an appropriate location and attentive care. After all, it is not always insect pests or diseases, but sometimes simply adverse growing conditions that keep a plant from flourishing. An overcrowded container or a location that doesn't receive enough sunlight can make plants more vulnerable to pests and diseases, as can too much (or too little) water or fertiliser (see the sections on "Location" and "Care").

Take the time to check your plants regularly, even the undersides of the leaves. Aphids, thrips, spider mites and other insects are easy to spot with the naked eye or with a magnifying glass. Fungi, bacteria and viral diseases are somewhat more difficult to recognise, but the organism can usually be identified by the damage it causes. You can increase your plants' resistance to pests and diseases with so-called plant tonics. They contain numerous important compounds which strengthen plant tissues and make them more resistant to pathogens.

Combating Pests

If, despite all preventive measures, an infestation occurs, the first course of action is to move the affected plant as far as possible from your other plants. Remove any heavily affected parts of the plant immediately, and thoroughly clean the area where the afflicted plant was standing. This will prevent your other, healthy plants from becoming infected. Frequently, the plant itself will tolerate a limited number of pests without suffering any real damage. However, if combatting pests becomes un-avoidable, there are several environmentally friendly approaches you can take:

- **Beneficial insects** such as ladybugs, lacewings or hoverflies can devour large numbers of pests. When you avoid the use of chemical pesticides as much as possible, these insects can make their homes on your balcony.
- You can order commercially marketed **bene-ficial organisms** for use in your home. Among those available are predatory mites that attack spider mites; gall midge and lacewing larvae, which feed on aphids; ichneumon flies, which live on white fly larvae; and assassin bugs, which primarily feed on thrips.
- Some pests are attracted to blue or yellow **glue-coated strips** which allow you to diagnose the infestation early and catch the insects at the same time. These strips can be used in enclosed spaces and are also available in shops.

- In non-sensitive, hard-leafed (sclerophyllus) plants, pests will often disappear if you shower the plant vigorously with lukewarm water or dip it, upside down, in a **soft soap solution.** This is easy to mix: dissolve 20 g (2/3 oz) pure soft soap in 1 litre (1 pint) warm water, then spray or rub the plant with the solution. If the infestation is severe, ask a specialist in a garden store to recommend a pest control solution that can safely be used indoors. Options include **oil solutions**, which create a film under which scale insects and mealybugs suffocate, potash soap-based solutions, or ready-made herbal preparations.
- **Leaf shine spray** works like an oil solution, suffocating sucking pests. Used with care; not all plants tolerate these sprays.
- A **cold water extract of stinging nettle** helps ward off aphids. Soak 1 kg (2 lb) fresh or 200 g (8 oz) dried stinging nettles in 10 litres (9 quarts) water. Stir the brew daily and spray on plants, undiluted, after one to two days.
- **Tansy broth** is effective against aphids, spider mites and fungal diseases. Soak 300 g (11 oz) fresh or 30 g (1 oz) dried plant parts in 10 litres (9 quarts) water for 24 hours; then boil the mixture for 20–30 minutes. Cool the solution and spray on affected plants.
- **Horsetail grass tea** helps cure fungal diseases such as mildew, rust or scurf. Add 1 kg (2 lb) fresh or 150 g (5 oz) dried herb to 10 litres (9 quarts) water; boil for 30 minutes. Strain the tea and dilute it with water at a ratio of 1:5; spray on plants.

Insect Pests

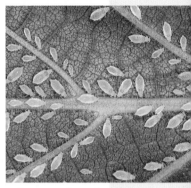

Aphids: The sucking activity of these pests can result in stunted young shoots and crumpled leaves. The young, tender parts of the plant are most vulnerable. Aphids secrete sticky substance called "honeydew" on which sooty moulds grow, and the plant wilts. In addition, aphids can carry dangerous viral diseases. *Remedy:* Balanced fertilising will prevent the growth of soft, vulnerable shoots; any affected parts should be removed. In case of severe infestations apply soft soap solution, stinging nettle extract or an insecticide that is not harmful to beneficial organisms – or introduce beneficial insects.

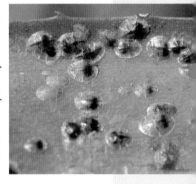

Scale insects: These flat or rounded, yellow to brownish lice sit motionless on branches and leaves. Due to the honeydew they secrete, sooty moulds almost always follow an infestation. *Remedy:* You can only remove a few of the insects easily by hand; otherwise, it is best to use a soft soap solution or, in the case of hard-leafed plants, an oil solution. Ichneumon flies are the natural enemies of scale insects; you can order them from shops for use in your home.

Mealybugs: These small, moving lice are coated with a white, waxy secretion. They especially like sucking on leaf axils. Sooty moulds often develop in the honeydew they secrete.

41

Remedy: The same as for scale insects. In order to curb the mealybugs' reproduction, do not keep vulnerable plants overly warm in the winter.

Spider mites: These minute creatures – just 0.5 mm long – usually suck on the underside of leaves, causing light-coloured dots to appear on the leaf surface. The leaves then dry out and die off. They frequently spin white webs between the leaf axils and the undersides of the leaves. Dry, warm (indoor) air can encourage particularly heavy infestations. *Remedy:* Increase the humidity and shower your plants more often; apply soft soap solution or an insecticide that doesn't harm beneficial organisms; introduce predatory mites.

White flies: These tiny white "moths" and their larvae sit on the underside of leaves. If you touch the leaf, the adult insects immediately fly off. Yellow speckles appear on the leaf surfaces; the leaves dry out and fall off. Sooty moulds develop in the honeydew the flies secrete. *Remedy:* Use a fertiliser low in nitrogen; otherwise the plant will become soft and vulnerable. Keep rooms well ventilated. If necessary, hang yellow glue strips to check for infestation. If the plants are heavily affected, apply an insecticide that doesn't harm beneficial organisms, or introduce ichneumon flies.

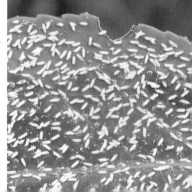

Thrips: These pests leave shiny, silvery marks where they have sucked on leaves and petals, which later become brown and dry. Leaves dry out and die off and the plant grows poorly overall. The insects frequently suck from the underside of the leaves. *Remedy:* Avoid moist locations and high humidity. Hang coloured glue strips to check for infestation and to capture the pests. If the infestation is heavy, apply an insecticide that won't harm beneficial organisms. Assassin bugs, thrips' natural enemies, can be ordered from garden shops. Do not throw infested plants into the compost bin, since the pests can survive there.

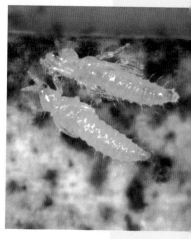

Vine weevils: If irregular notches appear on the edges of leaves, vine weevils have surely been nibbling there. This pest is not only active in the evening; during the day it lives below ground. The small white larvae devour the roots of a plant, causing it to wilt and grow poorly. *Remedy:* The adult beetles can be captured; you can purchase parasitic nematodes which can simply be spread on the ground to eat the larvae.

Springtail (collembola): These tiny white insects feed on roots and stems; however, they are only dangerous in large numbers. When you water plants you can see them "hop" on the surface of the substrate. *Remedy:* Immerse the earth ball in water and collect any insects that emerge; keep the soil dry.

43

Cicadas: Damage is similar to that caused by spider mites. Cicadas and their larvae also suck on the undersides of leaves, leaving white speckles on the surface. However, the yellow-green cicadas jump off immediately if you touch the plant. Froghoppers or spittlebugs usually sit on the plant shoots and surround themselves with saliva-like foam. *Remedy:* Don't use fertilisers that are high in nitrogen; choose a well ventilated location. Apply stinging nettle extract; in case of heavy infestations, you may have to resort to a pesticide that doesn't harm beneficial organisms.

Shield bugs: These green to brownish, extremely nimble insects suck on plants' leaves, creating yellow spots which later turn brown and tear. Affected leaves look completely perforated. Shield bugs will also attack the tender buds of roses. This animal typically has a flat body with a triangular shield on its back. *Remedy:* Encourage this pest's natural enemies (birds); or spray with soft soap solution or a potash soap mixture (ideally early in the morning).

Plant Diseases

Grey rot (botrytis blight): This decaying fungus produces greyish-white, fuzzy mould on leaves, flowers and stems. It is particularly severe when the weather is warm and moist. *Remedy:* Do not place plants too close together, and avoid fertilisers that are high in nitrogen. Remove dead parts of the plant immediately.

Parasitic rust diseases: These fungi are particularly apparent on the underside of leaves, appearing as pustule-like, yellowish to rust-brown, dust-producing spore deposits; on the top of leaves they appear as yellow spots. The leaves dry out, and the plant grows poorly. *Remedy:* Reduce humidity and do not allow the leaves to be constantly moist; avoid excessive nitrogen fertiliser. Remove the parts of the plant where spores are present and destroy them, since the spores can survive. Extracts of tansy or horsetail grass help strengthen plants.

Powdery mildew can be identified by a floury-white coating usually found on the surface of leaves, on flower calyxes and young, tender shoots. The leaves turn brown and dry out. There are several different pathogens, many specific to certain plant species. *Remedy:* These fungi occur most frequently when warm, sunny days combine with dewy nights. Again, keep plants in a well ventilated location and avoid fertilisers with excessive nitrogen. Horsetail grass or tansy extracts help strengthen plants; in severe cases, you can apply a sulphur solution.

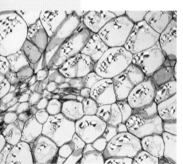

Downy mildew or pseudo mildew: Typical symptoms include pale purple to red-violet spots bordered by leaves' veins. Whitish or brownish spore deposits appear in the same places on the leaf undersides, resembling a powdery coating. The pathogens are frequently specific to particular plant species. *Remedy:* Cool, moist weather encourages mildew attacks, so avoid high humidity and moist substrate, and keep rooms well ventilated. Destroy any affected leaves or entire plants, since the fungus can survive on them.

Leaf spot: Various pathogens can cause dark, round spots to appear on leaves, particularly during long damp periods or when the leaves are frequently moist. The spots sometimes have red or purple edges, and black fruit bodies may appear on them as well. *Remedy:* Avoid high humidity and injuries to the plant. Do not place plants too close together and use low-nitrogen fertilisers. Remove any affected plants promptly. Horsetail grass solutions can help prevent leaf spot.

Sooty mould: This fungus appears as a black deposit in honey-dew, a sticky fluid that is secreted by many pests. Affected plants grow poorly. *Remedy:* Combat sucking insects that secrete honeydew (e. g. aphids); wipe off the deposits.

Root and stem rot: The plants wilt, even though the soil is moist. Roots and the bases of shoots rot, and leaves are a dull grey. *Remedy:* Do not keep plants overly moist; avoid standing water; and destroy any diseased plants.

Viral diseases: These diseases are caused by various pathogens, which are usually specific to a particular species. Typical symptoms include disrupted growth combined with mosaic-like, sharply defined spots on leaves and flowers, deformation of certain plant parts and the dying off of affected tissues. *Remedy:* Combat carriers of viruses, for example, aphids. Purchase plants that are healthy, and whenever possible, virus-resistant. Pay special attention to cleanliness when propagating plants (disinfect all tools and use sterile substrate).

Bacterial diseases: Depending upon the specific pathogen afflicting your plants, symptoms may include spotty leaves, galls, slimy rot, stem and root rot or withering diseases. *Remedy:* Immediately remove and destroy any affected plants.

47

Abutilon hybrids

FLOWERING MAPLE

Family Mallows *(Malvaceae)*

Origin The approximately 150 *Abutilon* species are native to South America. Hybridisation has created a wide variety of types.

Characteristics These shrubs, which grow up to 1.5 m (5 ft) in height, are also known as velvetleaf or Indian mallow. The bell-shaped flowers – white, yellow, orange or red, depending on the type – are produced throughout the summer. If the plant is

placed in a winter garden, it will bloom almost year round. In addition to the flowers, the maple-shaped green or coloured foliage is also very decorative.

Location Whether indoors or out, the plant prefers a bright, warm location away from direct midday sun. Protect the shrub from wind and frost. In order to bloom abundantly in summer, it requires temperatures of at least 15 °C (59 °F). Its winter location needs to be bright and at least 10 °C (50 °F); otherwise, the plant will lose its leaves.

Watering and fertilising Flowering maples require abundant water from spring until the end of summer. The substrate should never be allowed to dry out; therefore, it is best to place the pot in a saucer that can be refilled with water as needed. Fertilise the plant weekly during this period. Reduce both water and fertiliser at the end of the summer. Water only sparingly in the winter in order to avoid botrytis blight.

Care Re-pot the flowering maple every spring in nutrient-rich flower or houseplant soil. The new pot should not be too much bigger than the old one. To encourage more attractive branching, pinch off the tops of young plants. In older specimens, cut new shoots back by one third.

Propagation Top cuttings can be made in spring or summer; cultivate them at about 20 °C (68 °F). Sowing seeds in late winter at temperatures around 22 °C (72 °F) is possible, but tedious.

Acalypha hispida

CHENILLE PLANT

Family Spurges (*Euphorbiaceae*)

Origin This shrub – also known as red-hot cattail or foxtail – is native to the tropical regions of the Earth. With approximately 450 species, the genus is quite extensive.

Characteristics The most striking characteristic of the chenille plant – which grows to 50 cm (20 in) – is the red flower head, up to 50 cm (20 in) long, which give it its name. These appear throughout the summer and contrast attractively with the large, dark green, oval leaves. The 'Alba' variety has greyish-white flowers. With its overhanging growth pattern, *A. hispaniolae* works well as a hanging plant. Its flower heads are ca. 15 cm (6 in) long.

Location Bright and warm, but not direct sunlight. The plant develops best at temperatures of 20 °C (68 °F) and higher. During the winter rest period, temperatures should not drop below 16–18 °C (61–64 °F). If the air is too dry, the plant will react by rolling up its leaves. Keep it sheltered from wind.

TIP

The ideal location for Acalypha hispida *is an enclosed plant window where the humidity is high.* A. hispaniolae, *on the other hand, will also flourish well on a balcony in the summertime.*

Watering and fertilising Use a sensitive touch regarding watering, as the chenille plant tolerates overly dry soil and standing water equally poorly. The plant rots easily if it is too wet. Fertilise weekly from spring until autumn; not at all in winter.

Care Chenilles should only be planted outdoors in warm regions with minimum temperatures of 15 °C (59 °F). Re-pot every year in the springtime, using high-quality potting soil.

Propagation Take top cuttings in the springtime and allow them to root at ca. 20 °C (68 °F). Planting several cuttings in one pot will create a bushy plant. Pinch off the top to allow for better branching.

! *Caution: Poisonous and/ or allergenic*

Adiantum raddianum

MAIDENHAIR FERN

Family Maidenhair ferns *(Adiantaceae)*

Origin Comprising approximately 200 species, this genus is prevalent throughout the world. The triangular-shaped maidenhair fern originally comes from the tropics of South America.

Maidenhair fern *Adiantum raddianum*

Characteristics This delicate-looking fern can grow to 50 cm (20 in) high. Its frond-like, green pinnae are striking against the extremely fine, black leaf stems. The 'Variegatum' variety has white-striped leaves; in the 'Brillantelse', they are golden yellow.

Location Semi-shady to shady. The fern's ideal environment has a temperature of 20–25 °C (68–77 °F) throughout the year, at 60 per cent relative humidity. In the summer, this might be a wind-sheltered balcony. Avoid temperatures below 7 °C (45 °F).

Watering and fertilising Keep the soil constantly moist; do not allow it to dry out, even in winter. At the same time, avoid standing water and use only soft, room temperature water. During the summer months, fertilise this salt-sensitive fern every 2 weeks with a lime-free fertiliser at one-half concentration.

Care If you remove any old fronds, the fern will grow back more fully. Normally, it is only necessary to re-pot every two years in slightly acid soil – for example, in a mixture of standard potting soil and peat or azalea substrate. Ferns can be re-planted in the same pot, since its roots prefer cramped conditions.

Propagation In the springtime, divide the rhizomes or sow the spores in a covered propagating case at 22–24 °C (72–75 °F). The spores are located on the undersides of the leaves; at the mature stage, they are brown. To harvest the spores, wrap the leaf in paper and place it in a warm, dry place for two to three days until the spores fall off by themselves.

Aechmea fasciata

SILVER VASE BROMELIAD

Family Pineapples (*Bromeliaceae*)

Origin The nearly 180 species are at home in the tropics of South America; *A. fasciata* originally comes from Brazil. In nature, this shrub – like all bromeliads – grows as an epiphyte on trees, where it receives its nutrients from the rainwater that collects in its funnel. It is also commonly called urn plant.

Characteristics The funnel-shaped rosette is made of ten to twenty leaves, green with white stripes, each up to 40 cm (15 in) long, and studded with thorns along the edges. From July to December, the plant produces an inflorescence ca. 35 cm (14 in) long, which bears long-lasting pink spathes. The actual blue flowers are located between the spathes and wither very quickly.

Location Bright, but no direct sunlight. In summer and winter, the minimum temperature should be 18 °C (64 °F); avoid radical changes in temperature. Relative humidity of 60 per cent is ideal.

NOTE *The silver vase bromeliad can tolerate the low humidity of our homes, but it is then quite susceptible to spider mites.*

Watering and fertilising Keep the substrate moderately moist, and in the summer, the funnel should always be kept filled with water. Avoid standing water. Supplement once a month in the spring and summer with a low dose of fertiliser (0.1 per cent concentration); pour the solution into the funnel as well.

Silver vase bromeliad *Aechmea fasciata*

Care Mist the plant on warm days. Re-pot every three years in the springtime. It is important to use a loose, coarse substrate with a low pH value (e. g. special bromeliad substrate).

Propagation In the springtime, you can separate any offshoots containing roots from the parent plant and continue cultivating them at temperatures of 20–25 °C (68–77 °F).

Agave americana
CENTURY PLANT

Family Agaves (*Agavaceae*)

Origin The maguey, or American aloe, as this species is also called, originally comes from Mexico and has been naturalised into the Mediterranean regions.

Characteristics The century plant grows in a rosette formation, with blue-green leaves that grow up to 1.75 m (6 ft) in length. They have serrated edges and sharp thorns at their tips.

In addition to this species, there are varieties with variegated leaves: 'Marginata' has leaves with yellow edges, while those of 'Marginata alba' are white – even pink in young plants. 'Medio-picta' has a bright yellow centre stripe; 'Stricta' has white or yellow-striped leaves.

To reduce the risk of injury, trim off the sharp end thorns or cover them with corks.

TIP

Location Century plants like a sunny to slightly shady location; they may be placed outdoors in the summer, but should be protected from rain. Older specimens require a great deal of space. Keep the plant in a bright location in winter, at approximately 5 °C (41 °F); the root ball should remain nearly dry. If the humidity is too high, the leaves will become soft and droop over.

Watering and fertilising This succulent does not need a great deal of water and can survive dry periods well. Water only when the substrate is dried out; in winter, only if the plant begins to wither. A supplement of cactus fertiliser every four weeks in summer is recommended.

Care If the plant outgrows its pot, re-pot it in the springtime in sandy soil, such as cactus substrate. It is a good idea to include a drainage layer of clay potshards or similar material.

Propagation Separate offshoot rosettes when re-potting and re-plant them in fresh substrate.

Anigozanthos
KANGAROO PAW

Family Bloodworts (*Haemodoraceae*)

Origin Western Australia. The best-known varieties are *Anigozanthos flavidus*, the hardy large kangaroo paw; and *A. manglesii*, the 'Mangle's' kangaroo paw, with its lance-shaped leaves. A wide range of hybrid varieties are also available commercially.

Characteristics This exotic-looking perennial forms a ground-level rosette with its long, lance-shaped leaves. In the case of *A. flavidus*, the flower stalks can grow up to 1.5 m (5 ft) high. At the ends of the stalks are the tube-shaped flowers, whose colours vary from pink to yellowish to greenish, and which supposedly resemble the paws of a kangaroo. At 80 cm (31 in), *A. manglesii* is smaller; its yellowish-green flowers grow on the ends of red flower stems. In the kangaroo paw's natural habitat, the flowers appear in the springtime; in our climate, the plants tend to bloom in the warm summer months.

Location Sunny; on the terrace or balcony in the summer. In winter the plant prefers a bright and well ventilated location at approximately 10–15 °C (50–59 °F).

Watering and fertilising Water liberally in the summer, but avoid standing water and do not let the leaves remain moist. Otherwise, they may be prone to leaf spot disease. If the substrate is allowed to dry out, the plant will lose its buds. It is best to use soft water, such as rainwater. Fertilise in small doses every two weeks during the growing period.

58

Care Re-pot in the summer using ordinary potting soil mixed with bark substrate, sand or gravel for good drainage. Cut off wilted blossoms regularly. Older plants will often appreciate an occasional thinning.

Propagation You can divide the rhizomes when re-potting. It is also possible to sow seeds at room temperature; they will germinate year round.

59

Anthurium andraeanum
LARGE FLAMINGO FLOWER

Family Arum lilies *(Araceae)*

Origin This genus comprises well over 500 species, which originate in the tropical regions of the Americas. In its native Colombia, this species grows as a shrub, as does its little sister, *A. scherzerianum.*

Characteristics The large flamingo flower can grow to 1 m (3 ft) high. Its large, shiny green leaves are heart-shaped and grow on the ends of long stems. The striking spathe surrounding the flower spadix may be red, white or salmon-coloured, according to the variety. This species blooms throughout the year.

Location Bright to semi-shady; avoid direct sunlight. The location should not be too dark in the winter. In summer, temperatures of 20–22 °C (68–72 °F) or higher are ideal; it should not fall below 16 °C (61 °F) in winter. The relative humidity should be at least 70 per cent.

Watering and fertilising This plant requires abundant water in the summer months; it should be kept constantly moist. Do not water too much in the winter, however, or the roots can easily rot. Use only softened, room temperature water. Fertilise every two weeks in the spring and summer.

Care Since the large flamingo flower requires very high humidity, try to mist it daily. Be careful not to wet the spathes, or unattractive spots will appear. Re-pot every two years in a loose, slightly acidic substrate, such as azalea or orchid soil.

Propagation Older shrubs can be divided in spring; the new plants will bloom after one to two years. Work very carefully, so as not to injure the delicate roots. Seedlings need to mature for several years before producing their first flowers. Professionally cultivated *anthuriums* are usually propagated via tissue culture.

Anthurium scherzerianum

SMALL FLAMINGO FLOWER

Family Arum lilies *(Araceae)*

Origin The small flamingo flower, or tail flower, is native to Costa Rica and Guatemala.

Characteristics At ca. 50 cm (20 in) high, *A. scherzerianum* is clearly smaller than the large flamingo flower. Its lancet-shaped leaves are more delicate, and its swivelled flower spadix is striking. The spathes range from flaming red or red-and-white speckled to salmon-coloured or orange. This plant blooms once a year, often between January and May, bearing more flowers than the larger species.

NOTE

Foliage anthuria are no less attractive than their large-flowered relatives. A. crassinervium, for example, is very decorative, bearing large heart-shaped leaves with light-coloured veins that stand out strikingly from the dark green leaf colour.

Location and care See *Anthurium andraeanum*. With appropriate care, anthuriums can grow well in a warm front room. However, they will flourish luxuriantly in an enclosed plant window with a warm, moist climate that approximates that of their homeland.

! *Caution: Poisonous and/or allergenic*

ZEBRA PLANT

Family Acanthus or black-eyed Susans (*Acanthaceae)*

Origin This semi-shrub originates in south-eastern Brazil.

Characteristics The zebra plant's egg-shaped leaves, 20–30 cm (8–12 in) long, are dark green with striking silvery-white patterns along the veins. The flower heads – made up of brilliant yellow flowers and spathes – open from bottom to top and last a very long time. Blooming plants are available nearly all year round.

Location Bright, but without direct sun. Temperatures of 18–22 °C (64–72 °F) in summer; at least 18 °C (64 °F) in winter. Avoid draughts or drastic changes in temperature; be sure that the air is sufficiently moist. If the plant is too cold or too wet, it will lose its leaves.

Watering and fertilising Keep the soil slightly moist in summer; water less in wintertime. Fertilise weekly from spring through autumn; once a month in the winter.

Care Re-pot every 1–2 years in the spring.

Propagation Make cuttings of tender new growth in the spring or summer and root them at soil temperatures of ca. 25 °C (77 °F).

Ardisia crenata

CORAL ARDISIA

Family Myrsines *(Myrsinaceae)*

Origin This species is at home in South-east Asia, where it grows wild as a shrub or small tree. It is also called coralberry, spice berry or hen's eyes.

Characteristics This evergreen plant, which grows to 60–120 cm (24–48 in), has leathery leaves with wavy notches along the edges. The small nodes host bacteria that live in a symbiotic relationship with the plant. From summer to autumn, white or pink flowers appear in thick panicles just below the foliage crown. These develop into gleaming red and very long-lasting berries.

TIP
You can encourage fruit development by dusting the flowers with a small paintbrush.

Location Bright; preferably morning sun. A moderately warm room with temperatures of 18–20 °C (64–68 °F) in the summer is ideal; in winter, 16–18 °C (61–64 °F). A relative humidity of at least 60 per cent is necessary to maintain the berries.

Watering and fertilising Keep the earth ball slightly moist all year round. Fertilise every two weeks during the growing period; in winter, not more than every four weeks.

Care Regular misting is recommended to maintain a constant level of humidity. Re-pot every 1–2 years in the springtime in loamy flower soil.

Propagation If you wish to propagate your coral ardisia your-self, remove the seeds from the berries, rinse them in a sieve and allow to dry thoroughly. They require temperatures around 25 °C (77 °F) to germinate; the best time to do so is in the spring. Alternatively, you can take young to semi-mature top cuttings in the summer and cultivate them at 25 °C (77 °F).

Argyranthemum frutescens

SUMMER DAISY

Family Daisies, composite flowers (*Asteraceae*)

Origin This species is native to the Canary Islands.

Characteristics Depending upon the variety, summer daisies can grow between 40 and 80 cm (15–31 in) high. Their natural growth pattern is bushy; however, they lend themselves well to

high-stemmed cultivation. Since these plants are sensitive to frost, they are frequently grown as annuals in our climate. Their inflorescence covers the fine, feathery foliage throughout the summer. They consist of yellow disk flowers in the centre surrounded by white, yellow or pink ray florets, depending upon the variety, which may be single or compound.

Location Sunny and protected from wind to avoid damage to the delicate foliage. If you move the plant into a winter garden in the autumn, it will continue to bloom.

Watering and fertilising Summer daisies require a great deal of water, particularly on hot days, when you may even need to water twice. Plants that are wintered over should be watered less; however, do not allow the root ball to dry out. To ensure abundant blossoms, fertilise the plant once a week from spring until the end of summer.

Care If you regularly cut off wilted flowers, the plant will continue to bloom uninterrupted. To winter the plants over, place them in a bright location with temperatures between 5 and 15 °C (41–59 °F), depending on the available light. Good ventilation will help prevent botrytis blight. Spring is the best time for a moderate shaping trim or a radical pruning. If your wintering-over space is limited, you can also prune in the autumn.

Propagation Top cuttings taken in spring grow best at 16–18 °C (61–64 °F). Pinch off the tops regularly to encourage full growth.

Asclepias currassavica

RED BUTTERFLY WEED

Family Milkweeds (*Asclepiadaceae*)

Origin This evergreen semi-shrub is a native of the American tropics; it is also called scarlet milkweed or bloodflower.

Characteristics The bushy plants grow approximately 1 m (3 ft) high. The lancet-shaped leaves are green on the surface and blue-green on the undersides; depending on their location, they may even have a reddish colour. From the early summer into autumn thid plant produces thick umbels whose individual flowers are made up of a yellow "crown" and orange to dark red petals. The umbels develop into a long fruit pod, which contains a large number of seeds and is covered with shiny, silky hair.

TIP
The flower stalks make long-lasting cut flowers.
Since they contain a milky sap, dip the cut edge
in hot water for approximately one minute.

Location As sunny and warm as possible; avoid frost in winter.

Watering and fertilising Red butterfly weed requires a great deal of water during the blooming period, but it is generally better to keep it too dry rather than too moist, as its roots and stems rot easily. Water wintered-over plants only occasionally. Fertilise once a week from spring to late summer. If the winter quarters are very bright at temperatures of 10–12 °C (50–54 °F), the plant will produce new growth quickly in the springtime.

Red butterfly weed *Asclepias currassavica*

Care Re-pot if necessary in the springtime, using a nutrient-rich substrate. Prune the plant back slightly in spring.

Propagation Sow seeds – either purchased or self-harvested – from late winter, at 15–20 °C (59–68 °F). Pinch off the tops of young plants several times to encourage good branching.

❗ *Caution: Poisonous and/or allergenic*

ASPARAGUS FERN

 Family Asparagus (*Asparagaceae*)

 Origin This extensive genus consists of more than 300 species, whose natural habitat ranges from tropical to southern Africa. In addition to *A. falcatus* – which is also found in Sri Lanka – *A. densiflorus*, with its thickly branching, overhanging shoots is a well known plant for pots or hanging baskets.

Characteristics

Thanks to its thorny sprouts, this shrub is also known as sickle-thorn asparagus. It is distinguished by its dark green, sickle-shaped pseudo-leaves (so-called cladophylls), which are in fact tiny, leaf-like stems. This fern has slightly over-hanging branches that can grow to be several metres long; the incon-spicuous flowers make their appearance in July and August.

Asparagus fern *Asparagus falcatus*

Location The asparagus fern likes a bright location, but away from the direct sun. During the summer months – when the plant is also very happy outdoors – the temperature should be around 20 °C (68 °F); in the winter, it requires temperatures of at least 16–18 °C (61–64 °F). Since asparagus flourishes in high humidity, it will also do well in a bathroom.

> *If the plant loses its leaves, its location may be too sunny, or it may be receiving too much water or fertiliser.*

TIP

Watering and fertilising It is important to water this plant regularly and not allow the substrate to dry out. If the relative humidity is low, mist the plant frequently. The asparagus fern requires a dose of fertiliser every two weeks during the vegetation period; in the winter, fertilising once every two months is sufficient.

Care Asparagus ferns are relatively low maintenance. Nevertheless, you should treat your plant to a new pot and fresh substrate in the springtime.

Propagation You can divide larger specimens in the spring. Alternatively, you can sow seeds in late winter at approximately 20°C (68 °F); however, the seeds must be kept in the dark until they germinate.

Aspidistra elatior

CAST IRON PLANT

Family Lily of the valley family *(Convallariaceae)*

Origin This species, which is also known as bar room plant, originally comes from China and has been naturalised in Japan.

Characteristics Although it is sometimes referred to as a palm, the cast iron plant is actually a shrub. Its wide, leathery, dark green leaves can grow up to 70 cm (28 in) long and 10 cm (4 in) wide. The inconspicuous flowers appear at the base of the plant from February to April. The 'Variegata' variety is green and white striped.

Location This extremely robust plant can live almost anywhere; the only thing it will not tolerate is direct sunlight. Nor is the cast iron plant choosy about humidity or temperature as long as it remains above 2 °C (36 °F). 'Variegata', on the other hand, requires a bright, temperate location at temperatures of at least 10–12 °C (50–54 °F) to maintain its attractive patterns.

TIP

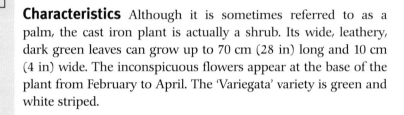

The cast iron plant is the right choice for difficult locations where many other plants grow poorly.

Watering and fertilising Keep the plant moderately moist during the summer months. In winter, water only when the soil is dry. Fertilise once a month from spring until autumn.

72

Cast iron plant *Aspidistra elatior*

Care The cast iron plant is very easy to care for. It requires little attention other than a dose of fertiliser at four-week intervals. Re-pot in high-quality potting soil every 2–3 years; the new pot should not be significantly larger than the old one. The cast iron plant tolerates dust, draughts and radical temperature changes.

Propagation Between March and May, cut the woody rhizome into sections containing two leaves each and replant them. The cultivating temperature should be around 15 °C (59 °F).

Asplenium nidus

BIRD'S NEST FERN

Family Spleenworts *(Aspleniaceae)*

Origin With over 700 species, the widely varied genus of nest ferns is at home in the tropical regions of the world.

Characteristics This decorative fern forms wide, solid, brilliant green fronds that are wavy along the edges. It generally grows about 30–40 cm (12–15 in) high as a houseplant; in nature it can

grow over 1 m (3 ft) in height. Its leaves form a funnel in which the plant collects water and nutrients. In its natural habitat, it grows on trees as an epiphyte, but produces its own food.

Location The best location is semi-shady, away from the direct rays of the sun. The temperature should be around 20–25 °C (68–77 °F); it should not fall below 16 °C (61 °F) in the winter. A corresponding ground temperature is also very important. The relative humidity should be around 60 per cent.

Keep an eye out for thrips, spider mites, and especially scale insects.

TIP

Watering and fertilising It is important to keep the substrate slightly moist at all times and to pour a little water into the rosette. Use only softened, lukewarm water. Mist the plant frequently to maintain high humidity. Fertilise at one-half concentration – once a month from spring until autumn, every two months in winter.

Care Re-pot every 2–3 years in the spring or summer. The ideal substrate is humus and slightly acidic, with a pH of around 5 (e. g. azalea substrate).

Propagation You can sow the ripened brown spores in the springtime in a mixture of peat and sand at 22 °C (72°F).

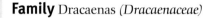

Beaucarnea recurvata

PONYTAIL PALM

Family Dracaenas *(Dracaenaceae)*

Origin This succulent shrub, also known as *Nolina recurvata*, is native to Mexico.

Characteristics This plant is also known by the common names bottle palm or elephant-foot tree. Its most striking characteristic is the ball-shaped swelling at the base of its trunk, which serves as a water storage tank. Growing in tufts at the end of the trunk are the narrow, up to 1-m (3-ft) long overhanging leaves. When well cared for, the ponytail palm can grow up to 2 m (7 ft) high in the home.

Location Sunny to bright and warm (20–25 °C/68–77 °F). The ponytail palm enjoys an outdoor location in the summer, but you should introduce it to the sunny conditions gradually. This frost-sensitive plant also requires a bright location in the winter; temperatures should not drop below 8 °C (46 °F).

Watering and fertilising Keep the substrate uniformly moist in summer, but do not allow standing water to build up; mist the plant with water frequently. In winter, water only when the soil is dry. Fertilise every two weeks during the growing period, preferably with a foliage fertiliser. If you re-pot the plant in the spring, it will not require any additional fertiliser that year.

Care Re-pot every 2–3 years in early spring, before the plant begins to grow, in loose flower soil or cactus substrate. The new

76

pot should be only slightly larger than the base of the trunk, and as flat as possible. A dish or bowl is very good for this purpose.

Propagation The ponytail palm sometimes develops offshoots, which can be separated and rooted in a mixture of peat and sand at 25 °C (77 °F), covered with plastic film. Seed propagation is extremely tricky.

ELATIOR BEGONIA

Family Begonias (*Begoniaceae*)

Origin The countless varieties of begonias are the products of various hybridisations. Another well known flowering begonia is the Lorraine begonia, whose white or pink blossoms are somewhat smaller but very abundant.

Characteristics This bushy plant grows out of a tuber. Its deep green leaves are asymmetrical in shape, with either smooth or fringed edges. The many varieties include both simple and compound flowers in nearly every colour. The begonia's natural blooming period is in the winter months, but systematic cultivation has made flowering specimens available throughout the year.

Location Bright, but without direct sunlight. In summer the ideal temperature is around 20 °C (68 °F); during the winter months it is 15–18 °C (59–64 °F). Elatior begonias enjoy a stay on the balcony during the warm seasons of the year.

If a plant loses its leaves, it may be due to too drastic temperature changes or a draughty location.

TIP

Watering and fertilising Keep the earth ball slightly moist at all times; avoid both standing water and drying out. Do not mist the plant. Fertilise every 1–2 weeks during the growing period.

Care Elatior begonias are generally kept for only one season. If you wish to continue cultivating a plant, re-pot it after the blooming period and prune back by one-third.

Propagation Take top cuttings in the spring and root them at a soil temperature of 20–22 °C (68–72 °F).

Begonia Rex hybrids

REX BEGONIAS

Family Begonias (*Begoniaceae*)

Origin The hybrid varieties are the result of crosses between *Begonia rex* (from Assam) and *B. diadema* (from Borneo).

Characteristics These foliage begonias' most eye-catching feature is their strikingly shaped and patterned leaves. They may, for example, be dark green with silver patterns, red with a black centre and black edges, or even tri-coloured – the range of types is enormous. The leaves are heart-shaped and pointed, with zigzag edges and a corrugated surface. Foliage begonias form rhizomes rather than tubers and as houseplants bloom only very seldom.

Location Bright to shady – a good choice for a north window. The optimum temperature is around 20–25 °C (68–77 °F); in winter the plant appreciates a somewhat cooler location. The relative humidity should be at least 60 per cent. Avoid draughts and radical temperature changes as much as possible.

Watering and fertilising Keep the soil uniformly moist with room temperature water, but do not allow standing water to form. Water less in the autumn and winter. Do not let the leaves remain wet. Supplement the plant once a week from spring until autumn, using a special foliage fertiliser; in winter, fertilise only once every six weeks.

Rex begonias *Begonia Rex* hybrids

Care Re-pot in ordinary potting soil every 1–2 years in the spring-time. If you prune the plant back, its growth will be bushier. Otherwise, the rex begonia is a hardy and easy-to-care-for plant.

Propagation Take a healthy leaf and cut off the leaf stem; cut through each main artery on the underside. Lay the leaf with the underside down in a dish filled with propagating soil; secure and keep moist at 20–25 °C (68–77 °F). In a few weeks, tiny plantlets will have developed. Alternatively, you can cut the leaf into small quarters which each contain one main artery.

Begonia Tuberhybrida group
TUBEROUS BEGONIAS

Family Begonias (_Begoniaceae_)

Origin The wild species from which today's varieties are descended have their origins in South America.

Characteristics Depending on the variety, these perennials may grow upright or hanging. The large flowers can be found in almost every colour and shape, simple or compound, smooth or wavy. They create a striking contrast to the asymmetrical, light to olive green leaves.

Location Semi-shady; protected from rain and wind, since the flower stalks break easily. Minimum temperature 10 °C (50 °F).

Watering and fertilising Water well during the blooming period, but avoid standing water. Fertilise once per week.

Care Remove any wilted blossoms in order to prolong the blooming period.

Propagation Dig up the tubers before the first frost; clean them, allow to dry and winter over at 5–7 °C (41–45 °F). Divide the tubers in spring and plant them in fresh, nutrient-rich substrate with the axil facing upward. Place the plants outdoors from mid-May. Propagation via seeds or cuttings is more difficult.

Bellis perennis

ENGLISH DAISY

Family Daisies, composite flowers (*Asteraceae*)

Origin English daisies (or lawn daisies) are at home in Europe and Asia Minor.

Characteristics These biennials, which grow approximately 15 cm (6 in) high, first form a rosette of elongated oval leaves; in early spring the colourful flower heads emerge. Depending on the variety, they may be white, pink or red, simple or compound; the flowers may be up to 5 cm (2 in) in diameter.

Location A sunny to semi-shady location on the balcony, patio, or garden.

Watering and fertilising The substrate should be rich in nutrients and should not be allowed to dry out. Since the blooming period is short, supplemental fertilising is not necessary.

Care Pinch off wilted flowers; otherwise, these plants are very undemanding.

Propagation Sow seeds in summer; cover lightly and keep moist. The best temperature for germination is 15–18 °C (59–64 °F). Separate individual plants and winter them over in a frost-free place.

Bougainvillea glabra

BOUGAINVILLEA

Family Four-o-clocks (*Nyctaginaceae*)

Origin Near the end of the eighteenth century, a French seaman named Bougainville introduced the gorgeously coloured paper flower – as the bougainvillea is also called – into the Mediterranean region from its homeland of Brazil. The flower has borne his name ever since.

Characteristics This climbing shrub with thorny shoots can grow to heights of 10 m (33 ft) or more when planted outdoors. However, since the plant is sensitive to frost, this is only possible in warm regions. In our climate it grows as a container plant and does not achieve such great heights. Instead, you can cultivate it as a bush, as a high-stemmed plant or on a trellis. The sturdy green leaves are elliptically shaped and pointed at the ends; the texture may be matte or shiny. Each of the small, white, tube-shaped flowers is surrounded by three striking spathes. The red and purple varieties are the best known, but white, yellow, orange and even compound types also exist. Depending upon its location, the bougainvillea can bloom nearly year round; the main blooming period extends from spring to early summer. The spathes lose their colour after the blooming period. One peculiarity of the *Nyctaginaceae* family is that the flowers do not open until nearly evening.

Location As sunny and warm as possible; well ventilated, but free of draughts. The plants can grow year-round indoors or in a winter garden; in the summer, as container plants outdoors.

84

Watering and fertilising During the blooming period, it is important to water liberally and uniformly. However, avoid standing water at all costs. Do not allow the root ball to dry out, or the plant will lose its leaves. Keep the soil drier in the winter. Fertilise once a week from spring through the end of summer.

Bougainvillea *Bougainvillea glabra*

Care In a light and temperate location (10–15 °C/50–59 °F) the plant will retain its leaves all winter and continue to bloom. In dark, cool winter quarters, it will lose its leaves and need minimal watering. Bougainvilleas respond well to pruning. You can cut large specimens back by about half before bringing them indoors; prune smaller plants just before new shoots begin to grow. Re-pot every two years; a loose, humus soil is important.

TIP

If you cut the long shoots back by one-fourth in the summer many new side branches will grow and produce buds.

Propagation You can take non-woody top and side cuttings throughout the year. However, they will root best in spring or summer when placed under plastic film at 25 °C (77 °F). It is helpful to add a rooting medium. Prop the young plants well to encourage good branching. For best results, plant several young plants together in one pot.

CALADIUM

Family Arum lilies *(Araceae)*

Origin The original species, C. *bicolor*, is native to Ecuador.

Characteristics This 40–60 cm (15–24 in) perennial has large, arrow-shaped leaves in a captivating array of colours; hence the name "fancyleafed caladium". The leaves dry out in winter.

Location As bright as possible, but no direct sunlight. Temperatures from 20 to 25 °C (68–77 °F) and high humidity are ideal. In winter, keep the plant dry at around 15–20 °C (59–68 °F).

Watering and fertilising Water generously with room temperature water during the growing period and fertilise once a week. Keep the humidity high, but do not allow the leaves to remain wet. Gradually keep the plant drier beginning in September.

Care Near the end of winter, clean the dry tuber and re-plant it in fresh, sandy and humus soil. At 20 °C (68 °F) or above and high humidity, the caladium will grow new shoots.

Propagation Remove any tuber offsets when re-potting and cultivate them as described above.

! *Caution: Poisonous and/or allergenic*

87

CALATHEA

Family Prayer plants or arrow roots (*Marantaceae*)

Origin The more than 150 species that make up this genus are all native to the tropical regions of the Americas; *C. crocata* has its origins in Brazil. In addition to this variety, *C. makoyana*, with strikingly patterned leaves up to 30 cm (12 in) long, is also a very popular houseplant.

Characteristics The flowers and leaves of this plant are equally attractive. The surface of the leaves is dark green; the undersides are reddish-brown. The flower stems – up to 20 cm (8 in) long – bear eye-catching orange-red blossoms at their tips.

Location Bright to semi-shady, out of direct sunlight. The ideal temperature range is 20–25 °C (68–77 °F); not below 16–18 °C (61–64 °F) even at night or in winter. A warm soil temperature helps the plant flourish. Be sure that the humidity is kept high.

TIP

The calathea will only produce flowers if it is kept in a darker location in the autumn. Therefore, it should not receive any light other than natural daylight during October and November.

Watering and fertilising Keep the substrate uniformly moist, but do not allow standing water to build up. Water somewhat less in the winter. Use only room temperature, softened water or rainwater. Mist the plant frequently, but avoid wetting the blossoms. Supplement with a fertiliser at one-half concentration

every two weeks during the summer (early July to late September). Plant damage is usually the result of overly low humidity or inappropriate watering.

Care Re-pot calatheas in the springtime in humus and slightly acidic potting soil – such as azalea substrate – or flower soil mixed with peat or a peat substitute. You may also wish to add a little expanded clay to the mix.

Propagation You can divide bushy specimens when re-potting in the springtime.

Calceolaria integrifolia

LADY'S SLIPPER

Family Figworts (*Scrophulariaceae*)

Origin The lady's slipper, also called slipperwort or pocketbook plant, comes from the mountains of Chile, where it is a semi-shrub. Since it is sensitive to frost, it is grown as an annual here.

Characteristics The plant grows bushy or compactly and reaches heights of 20–60 cm (8–24 in), depending on the variety. The unusually shaped flowers appear from May to September.

Lady's slipper *Calceolaria integrifolia*

They are double-lipped: the lower lip is puffed up and significantly larger than the upper one. The flowers may be yellow, red or brownish, a solid colour or speckled, and grow in clusters at the ends of the shoots. The bright colours of the blossoms form an attractive contrast to the light green, corrugated leaves.

Location Lady's slippers do well as houseplants, on a balcony or planted in the garden. They will grow in bright to semi-shady locations and prefer cool temperatures to those that are too hot. They are happiest at around 15–18 °C (59–64 °F). They enjoy a well ventilated location but will not tolerate draughts. Keep the plant protected from wind to prevent damage to the flowers.

Watering and fertilising Keep the soil moist during the blooming period, but don't pour water on the flowers. If the substrate has sufficient nutrients, supplemental fertilising is not necessary. Otherwise, fertilising once a month is enough.

Care If you regularly pinch off wilted flowers and seed stems, the plant will bloom continuously. Since the cultivation period is so short, there is no reason to re-pot.

Propagation You can sow seeds in late winter or summer. They require about two weeks to germinate, at temperatures of 15–18 °C (59–64 °F). Summer-germinated plants require a cool period in December to January, at approximately 8 °C (46 °F). You can also cultivate cuttings in the summer, placing them under plastic film at 20–22 °C (68–72 °F).

Calluna vulgaris
HEATHER

Family Heathers (*Ericaceae*)

Origin This evergreen shrub has its origins in the moors and heath lands stretching from northern and western Europe to Asia Minor.

Characteristics Depending upon the location, the bushy heather plant can grow to 20 cm (8 in) or higher. Beginning in late summer it displays its bell-shaped flowers, arranged in thick clusters at the ends of the shoots. Colours range from red or purple to pink or white, according to the type – even multi-coloured varieties are available. The blooming period extends from late summer until autumn. The narrow, needle-shaped leaves are dark to greyish green and frequently turn purplish in the winter. If you're looking for something very unusual, you can even find varieties with golden yellow or silver leaves.

NOTE

In the so-called bud-blooming varieties, the flowers do not open up. They remain very attractive until well into the winter months.

Location This classic plant is practically a must for a sunny to semi-shady autumn balcony.

Watering and fertilising Heather prefers moderately dry to moist conditions; as a moor garden plant, it requires an acidic, nutrient-rich, sandy substrate.

Care Cut back the wilted buds every year in the spring to encourage new flower growth. Fertilise the plant after pruning.

Propagation In the late summer and autumn, you can take semi-mature cuttings from non-blooming side branches. The cuttings should be approximately 5 cm (2 in) long and already have uniformly sized, thickly growing leaves. Root them at 15–20 °C (59–68 °F), airing the plants daily. Treat them prophylactically with a fungicide to prevent rotting moulds. Pinch off the tops of the rooted cuttings several times.

Camellia japonica

CAMELLIA

Family Teas *(Theaceae)*

Origin In its native countries of Japan, Korea and Taiwan the camellia grows as an evergreen shrub or tree.

Characteristics This bushy plant can grow up to 1.5 m (5 ft) tall in a container. Its elegant flowers appear from late autumn until springtime. Depending on the variety, they may be red, pink or white, simple or compound. They form a stunning contrast to the plant's shiny, dark green leaves.

Location Bright to semi-shady; avoid harsh sunlight. Camellias feel at home in cool rooms or winter gardens; in the summer, they are happy to stand on a patio or balcony. In order for the flower buds to mature, the temperature should not exceed 15 °C (59 °F). The cooler the temperatures during the blooming period, the longer the flowers will last. Keep the plant in a cool location (5–10 °C/41–50 °F) that is as bright as possible in the winter. Do not move the plant while the buds are developing.

Watering and fertilising Proper watering calls for a delicate touch. The substrate should be kept uniformly moist; avoid standing water or allowing the root ball to dry out. Keep the plant drier in winter and during the period when the buds are developing. Use only softened, lukewarm water, since camellias are sensitive to lime. Shower the plant occasionally until the buds begin to form. Fertilise once a week from spring to late summer, preferably with azalea fertiliser; later in the year, fertilise every two weeks at one-half concentration.

Care Give camellias a shaping trim immediately after the blooming period. Cut just above a bud, or at a side branch. Repot in azalea substrate after the blooming period every 2–4 years depending on the size of the pot.

Propagation Make cuttings in the late summer and root them in azalea substrate, covered over with plastic film, at 20–25 °C (68–77 °F). Prop young plants frequently.

Campanula isophylla

BELLFLOWER

Family Bellflowers *(Campanulaceae)*

Origin This small perennial is a native of northern Italy and is also frequently called Italian bellflower.

Characteristics The plant grows upright, about 20 cm (8 in) high, although the long shoots may hang over slightly. Thanks to its star-shaped flowers, which appear in midsummer, it is also called falling stars or star of Bethlehem. The flowers – which may be white or blue, depending on the variety – cover the rounded, fleshy green leaves almost entirely.

Location Whether indoors or out, bellflowers enjoy a bright to semi-shady, well ventilated location that is protected from harsh sunlight. They prefer cool temperatures to warm; the temperature should not be higher than 15 °C (59 °F) in winter.

TIP

> *Only this species is appropriate as a house or patio plant. It is particularly attractive in a hanging basket.*

Watering and fertilising Water only moderately, even during the growing and blooming periods. Fertilise twice a month at most. Hard water will not damage the plant.

Care It is important to move the plant indoors before the first frost. You can prune it back at this time, or do so when re-potting – in ordinary potting soil – in the spring. In winter, the

Bellflower *Campanula isophylla*

bellflower prefers a bright location and temperatures between 6 and 10 °C (43–50 °F). Water only when the substrate is dry. If the plant is too moist, it will be susceptible to fungi.

Propagation In spring you can propagate via seeds or take top cuttings, which will root at 10–15 °C (50–59 °F) under a plastic film cover. In order to create a bushy plant quickly, plant several young plants in one pot and pinch off the tops frequently. Larger plants may also be divided, preferably in spring or autumn.

Canna indica

INDIAN SHOT

Family Cannas (*Cannaceae*)

Origin The Indian shot or canna lily is at home in the West Indies and Central and South America, and has been naturalised in the tropics of Africa and Asia. There, the shrub grows primarily in marshy areas. Crossings of various species have produced a wide variety of hybrids.

Characteristics From summer until autumn, the creeping rootstock produces large oval leaves and flower shoots up to 1.5 m (5 ft) long. Depending on the variety, the leaves may be bright green, blue-green or red to bronze-coloured. The flowers, up to 10 cm (4 in) in diameter, are found in shades of red, pink, orange or yellow and resemble those of the gladiola.

Location This exotic container plant requires a very sunny and warm location on the balcony or patio, protected from the wind. Special dwarf varieties, which bloom from winter to spring, are available for indoor cultivation.

Watering and fertilising In summer this plant needs lots of water and nutrients. Water it liberally and fertilise once a week.

Care Remove wilted blossoms regularly. Cut the plant back to 10–20 cm (4–8 in) in the autumn; then dig up the rootstocks, clean them and store in either bright or dark conditions at 5–10 °C (41–50 °F). Keep the rootstocks dry; otherwise botrytis blight will set in quickly.

Propagation You can divide the dug-up rhizomes in late winter or spring. Each section must contain two or three axils. Powdering the cut edge or rubbing it with charcoal will prevent rotting. Plant the rhizomes at the end of the winter; place them in a bright location and pre-cultivate at 15–18 °C (59–64 °F).

Capsicum annuum

ORNAMENTAL PEPPER

Family Nightshades *(Solanaceae)*

Origin In the sixteenth century, Spanish sailors brought these plants to southern Europe from North, Central and South America. Thus, we sometimes hear the name Spanish pepper. Nowadays, the *Capsicum* genus includes a multitude of vegetable and ornamental varieties.

Characteristics The ornamental varieties have a bushy shape and are fairly compact at 20–25 cm (8–10 in) high. The inconspicuous flowers appear from summer to autumn, followed by the characteristic fruits, which are usually yellow or red, in striking contrast to the green, cone-shaped leaves.

Location Sunny to bright, without draughts. In the summer, ornamental peppers will flourish on a balcony and should be kept comfortably warm, at around 20 °C (68 °F). In winter 12–15 °C (54–59 °F) is sufficient.

Watering and fertilising Water generously to keep the fruits from shrivelling, but don't allow standing water to accumulate. Fertilise weekly in summer; every 2–3 weeks in winter.

Care Since this is an annual plant, there is no need to re-pot.

Propagation Sow seeds in early spring at ca. 20 °C (68 °F).

GREATER BROWN SEDGE

Family Sedges (*Cyperaceae*)

Origin This perennial grows in marshy areas and along bodies of water in South Asia and Australia.

Characteristics With its long, slender leaves, this upright-growing grass has a very delicate appearance. This species has green leaves; 'Variegata' is an eye-catching variety with yellow and green striped leaves.

Location Whether indoors or out, the best location is bright to semi-shady. The plant prefers a well ventilated spot that is free of draughts; from spring to autumn, it is comfortable at temperatures up to 25 °C (77 °F). In winter sedge likes a cooler (approx. 10 °C/50 °F) but frost-free location.

Watering and fertilising Keep the substrate evenly moist in the growing period, but if it remains wet the roots will rot. Fertilise every two weeks during this time. Water less in winter, but don't allow the substrate to dry out.

Care The sedge requires fresh soil every two years. Re-pot it at the same depth.

Propagation You can divide larger specimens at the time of re-potting.

Catharanthus roseus

MADAGASCAR PERIWINKLE

Family Dogbanes (*Apocynaceae*)

Origin This species comes from Madagascar and is related to the European common periwinkle (*Vinca*). In its natural habitat, it grows as an evergreen perennial. Cultivation has produced a number of varieties that are very popular as house and patio plants.

Characteristics The popularity of this 20-cm (8-in) high plant is largely due to its white, pink or purple flowers, which it produces tirelessly throughout the spring and summer. The leathery, dark green leaves with their light centre ribs are also highly decorative.

NOTE   *All parts of the periwinkle contain poisonous alkaloids, so be sure to keep the plant well out of the reach of children.*

Location The periwinkle prefers a sunny location, but will also tolerate semi-shade. Its ideal temperature is between 15 and 20 °C (59–68 °F). In summer, the frost-sensitive *catharanthus* is happy to have a place on the balcony.

Watering and fertilising Keep the substrate uniformly moist from spring through autumn; fertilise once per week. Watering should be reduced to a minimum in the winter. Avoid standing water at all costs.

Care If you wish to keep this hardy and easy-to-care for plant for more than one season, re-pot it at the end of winter in fresh, nutrient-rich potting soil and support its stems.

Propagation Sow seeds in spring at temperatures around 20 °C (68 °F). Keep these dark-germinating plants covered initially; once sprouted, place in a bright spot at around 15 °C (59 °F). Add supports regularly to encourage bushy growth. You can also take cuttings in spring or summer.

! *Caution: Poisonous and/ or allergenic*

Chamaedorea elegans

PARLOUR PALM

Family Palms *(Arecaceae, Palmae)*

Origin The dwarf mountain palm or love palm, as this species is also called, grows as a shrub in its native Mexico and Guatemala, reaching heights of 2–6 m (7–20 ft). It produces many runners and quickly forms a thick bush. *C. costaricana*, with its pretty, two-part pinnate leaves, is an equally beloved houseplant.

104

Parlour palm *Chamaedorea elegans*

Characteristics As a pot or container plant, this elegant palm can grow up to 100 cm (39 in) high. At the ends of its slender stems, multiple-feathered leaves grow in a tuft-like formation. Yellow flower buds may appear in spring and summer; however, they do not play a major role in the plant's development. Since the parlour palm is a monoecious plant, both male and female specimens are necessary for the formation of seeds.

Location Bright to semi-shady; the palm will even tolerate a north window. From spring to autumn, it prefers warm temperatures (20–25 °C/68–77 °F); in winter, 15 °C (59 °F) is sufficient. Ideally, the relative humidity should be around 50 per cent.

Watering and fertilising The earth ball should be kept slightly moist during the warm seasons. The plant appreciates frequent misting. Water less in the winter; however, the earth ball should not be allowed to dry out. Fertilise once a week during the growing period; once a month in winter.

Care If the parlour palm's pot becomes too crowded, re-pot it in the springtime, preferably using special palm substrate.

Propagation Sow seeds in the springtime under fairly warm (25–28 °C/77–82 °F) and humid conditions. Normally, it takes several months for the seeds to germinate. Planting several seeds in one pot will provide you with a bushy plant from the very beginning. If you prefer a faster method, you can carefully remove runners from the parent plant.

Chamaerops humilis
MEDITERRANEAN FAN PALM

Family Palms (_Arecaceae, Palmae_)

Origin Also called the European fan palm or dwarf fan palm, it is the only species in its genus and is native to Southern Europe.

Characteristics In their natural habitat these palms can grow up to 5 m (16 ft) high; in containers, they remain much smaller. They may have one stem or many; older potted specimens are most likely to develop a trunk. The stems of the deeply split, fan-like leaves have whitish thorns that can injure you. Yellow or orange-red blossoms may appear after several years of cultivation.

Location As sunny and well ventilated as possible, but free of draughts. The palm can be outdoors in summer, preferably where it is protected from rain. It tolerates both heat and light frost.

Watering and fertilising The Mediterranean fan palm does well in quite dry conditions and should be watered lightly, even in summer. To prevent rotting, avoid standing water or pouring water into the tufts of leaves. The plant should be kept even drier in winter. Add fertiliser to the water once a week when watering during the vegetation period; do not fertilise in winter.

Care Keep the fan palm in a frost-free location in winter. In a cool front room (at a maximum of 12 °C/54 °F), you will need to water occasionally. If necessary, the plant can also winter over in a cool, dark place (0–5 °C/32–41 °F), but let it gradually adjust to light in the spring. Re-pot about every three years in good-quality potting soil. A drainage layer – e. g. gravel, expanded clay or clay potshards – at the bottom of the pot is recommended.

Propagation If the palm develops offshoots, you can carefully remove them from the parent plant during re-potting and continue to cultivate them separately. Sow seeds in the spring when temperatures are at least 22 °C (72 °F).

Chlorophytum comosum

SPIDER PLANT

Family Grass lilies *(Anthericaceae)*

Origin This species originates in South Africa, where it grows as a perennial. It is a true classic among houseplants.

Characteristics The spider plant, which was previously classified in the lily family, goes by many names. It may also be referred to as ribbon plant, hen and chickens or airplane plant.

Its long, slender leaves grow in thick rosettes. Depending on the variety, they may be solid green, green-and-white or green-and-yellow striped. The spider plant develops long flower stems, which bear small white flowers on their ends in the summer. The last blossoms of the year develop into new plantlets.

Location This hardy plant will flourish in a bright to semi-shady location; the solid green varieties will even grow in the shade – for example, in a dimly lit stairwell. The spider plant's ideal temperature is between 20 and 25 °C (68–77 °F) year round but it does not suffer greatly if it is cooler (as low as 10 °C/50 °F). It grows well on the balcony during the summer.

Brown leaf tips are a sign of too-low humidity or standing water.

TIP

Watering and fertilising Keep the soil slightly moist, but not wet, at all times; otherwise the roots will rot. It is best to use softened, room temperature water. Supplement with fertiliser once a week from spring to early autumn; during the rest of the year, fertilise only every 3–4 weeks.

Care Re-pot as needed during the growing period, using regular potting soil. You can do this as often as once a year.

Propagation Separate plantlets that are not too small in the early summer. Plant them directly in propagating soil or allow them to root first in a glass of water. Larger plants may be divided.

109

Chrysalidocarpus lutescens

GOLDEN CANE PALM

Family Palms (*Arecaceae, Palmae*)

Origin This species, also called butterfly palm or bamboo palm, is a native of Madagascar. It is also known by the name Areca palm (*Areca lutescens*).

Characteristics In its natural habitat the golden cane palm can grow up to 15 m (16 ft); as a container plant it remains much smaller (approx. 2 m/7 ft). It normally has a single, short stem. The fronds, consisting of long, slender pinnae, fall gently apart.

Location Bright, but without harsh sunlight. The temperature should not dip below 16–18 °C (61–64 °F), and aim for a relative humidity of 60 per cent. In summer the palm can move from the living room to a sheltered location on a balcony or patio.

TIP

This decorative palm requires a fair bit of space in order to show itself to best advantage. It is well suited to a larger room or a winter garden, ideally in hydroponic culture.

Watering and fertilising The golden cane palm requires a great deal of water, not only in the summer months, so plan to water it regularly and thoroughly. The best solution is to place it in a saucer to which you regularly add a little water. If the substrate is allowed to dry out, unsightly spots will appear on the leaves. Mist the plant frequently. Fertilise once a week during the growing period.

110

Golden cane palm *Chrysalidocarpus lutescens*

Care If the palm's pot becomes too small, re-pot in the spring in a fresh, slightly acidic substrate.

Propagation Ground-level offshoots, which emerge from the rhizome, may be separated carefully in spring, planted in new pots and cultivated. Seeds can be sown any time of year; the temperature should be around 25 °C (77 °F). Keep in mind that the seeds generally take about four weeks to germinate.

Cissus rhombifolia
GRAPE IVY

Family Grapes (*Vitaceae*)

Origin This evergreen, climbing perennial is at home in Mexico, Central America and tropical South America.

Characteristics This lushly growing plant – which is also called rex begonia vine or tapestry vine – has particularly beautiful, three-part leaves which are dark green on the surface and

reddish and fuzzy on the underside. It will quickly add green to a trellis or even an entire wall, and is also eye-catching as a hanging plant. Its Australian relative, the kangaroo vine (*C. Antarctica*), has very large, egg-shaped leaves with edges serrated in a coarse, striking pattern.

Location Both species do well in bright to semi-shady locations at 10–20 °C (50–68 °F) and air that is not overly dry.

> *Larger specimens grow best in hydroponic*
> *culture, which makes re-potting unnecessary.*

TIP

Watering and fertilising Water uniformly, but do not allow standing water to accumulate. The amount of water should be tailored to the location – that is, the brighter and warmer the spot, the more water is needed. In the winter, water just enough that the substrate does not dry out. Add fertiliser to the water once a week from spring until autumn.

Care Re-pot every spring. If the plant becomes overly large, you can cut it back without reservations.

Propagation The best time to propagate via cuttings is in the late spring to early summer. Cuttings will take root very well in a glass of water or in propagating soil, covered with plastic film, at 20–25 °C (68–77 °F). Once they have taken root, support the young plants to encourage continued bushy growth.

CITRUS TREE

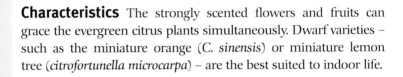

Family Rues (*Rutaceae*)

Origin Citrus plants are native to all tropical regions, and many have been naturalised into the Mediterranean region. The large family includes oranges, mandarin oranges and lemons.

Characteristics The strongly scented flowers and fruits can grace the evergreen citrus plants simultaneously. Dwarf varieties – such as the miniature orange (*C. sinensis*) or miniature lemon tree (*citrofortunella microcarpa*) – are the best suited to indoor life.

Location Bright to sunny. Container plants are happy to be outdoors in summer, at 18–25 °C (64–77 °F). Winter temperatures should be 10–15 °C (50–59 °F) and as bright as possible. Citrus plants need good ventilation, but do not tolerate draughts.

TIP *If standing water accumulates or the location is too warm in the winter, the plant will lose its leaves. Keep an eye out for scale insects and mealybugs.*

Watering and fertilising Keep citrus plants uniformly moist during the warmer months of the year, but be sure to use only softened water that has been allowed to stand. The plants should be kept substantially drier in the winter. Fertilise once a week from spring until autumn, ideally using an iron-fortified citrus fertiliser.

Care Citrus plants will only flourish with optimum care. It is sufficient to re-pot the plant every 2–4 years, preferably in a loose, loamy substrate that can store sufficient water. You can give container plants a shaping trim before you move them out of their winter quarters.

Propagation Home propagation is quite difficult. You can sow seeds that you harvest yourself; however, the plants will usually grow very large. Cuttings will root under a plastic film cover only if the soil is sufficiently warm (25–30 °C/ 77–86 °F) and a rooting medium is added. Gardeners typically graft particular species.

Clivia miniata
CLIVIA

Family Amaryllis (*Amaryllidaceae*)

Origin The clivia, also know as the Kaffir lily, is a native of the Natal region of South Africa. As a houseplant, it is a classic that has made a comeback in recent years.

Characteristics This shrub's strap-like leaves grow out of its fleshy rhizome and can reach lengths of up to 50 cm (20 in), spreading themselves like a fan. From late winter to early spring

the long (up to 80 cm/31 in) flower stem appears, bearing an umbel of orange, funnel-shaped flowers.

Location Bright to semi-shady, though it will tolerate direct sunlight in the morning or afternoon. Its location should also be warm (approx. 20 °C/68 °F) and well ventilated. Clivia can live on a balcony in summer, but blooming will be interrupted if it is moved frequently. Clivia will only develop flowers if kept in a cool (10–15 °C/50–59 °F), bright spot for two months in winter.

Watering and fertilising The soil should be kept slightly moist and never allowed to dry out, not even in the winter. As soon as buds appear, water liberally until summer. Now it is important to develop a sensitive touch, since the roots will rot if the plant is too wet. Watering with warm water (around 40 °C/104 °F) will encourage the flowers' development when they are beginning to open. Fertilise once a week from spring until autumn.

Care Re-pot as necessary, usually after two to three years. The best time to do so is after the blooming period. Use a sandy, porous substrate; clay pots are better than plastic.

Propagation Offshoots may form at the base of the plant, which you can separate and cultivate further on their own. Propagation via seeds is very tedious.

! *Caution: Poisonous and/or allergenic*

Codiaeum variegatum
CROTON

Family Spurges *(Euphorbiaceae)*

Origin Two varieties of variegated laurel, as the croton is also known – C. var. *pictum* and C. var. *variegatum* – originated in the Moluccan Islands of Indonesia. There the plants grow as shrubs or trees.

Characteristics The croton is a good example of a houseplant that can be decorative even without flowers. Depending on the variety its large, leathery leaves display colour combinations of green, yellow, orange or red. The shape of the leaves also varies widely – from broad to narrow, smooth-edged to wavy.

Location Bright to sunny, but out of the blazing midday sun. If the location is too dark, the leaves will turn green. The croton requires warm temperatures in the summer (20 °C/68 °F and above); in winter, temperatures should be kept between 15 and 20 °C (59–68 °F). Keep the relative humidity high – at least 60 per cent – and avoid radical changes in temperature.

Watering and fertilising Water regularly from spring until autumn and add a fertiliser every week. In winter, keep the soil only slightly moist and fertilise once a month at a low concentration. Use room temperature water.

Care Smaller plants need to be re-potted every year in spring-time; larger specimens should be re-potted every 2–3 years. A sandy, permeable substrate is very important.

Propagation Propagate via mossing (see page 36), or make cuttings from mature shoots in spring. These will only root in moist propagating soil, covered with plastic film in a bright location at 25–30 °C (77–86 °F). Since the plant contains a milky sap, you must allow the cut edge to dry before planting the cuttings.

! *Caution: Poisonous and/or allergenic*

Columnea

COLUMNEA

Family Gesneriads (*Gesneriaceae*)

Origin The three most common varieties for indoor cultivation are C. *gloriosa,* C. *microphylla* and C. *hirta,* which grow as evergreen shrubs or semi-shrubs in their home countries of Costa Rica and Honduras. Numerous hybrid varieties are now available.

Characteristics With its overhanging branches, which can grow up to 50 cm (20 in) long, columnea is an excellent choice for a hanging basket. Its small leaves are egg-shaped and may be solid

green or variegated with white, depending upon the variety. The large, orange to fiery red, tube-shaped flowers appear in the leaf axils in the spring, or in autumn for *C. gloriosa*. Thanks to the flowers' colour and shape, columnea is also known as the gold-fish plant.

Location Bright to semi-shady and sufficiently warm (at least 20 °C/68 °F) with high humidity. An enclosed plant window is an ideal location.

Watering and fertilising Keep the soil uniformly moist at all times, but do not allow standing water to accumulate. It is best to use softened water, preferably at room temperature; avoid wetting the leaves when watering. During the vegetation period, from spring to autumn, supplement with an acidifying fertiliser (e. g. azalea fertiliser) once a week; in winter, just once every four weeks is sufficient.

Care The best time to re-pot columnea is in early spring – once a year, if necessary. It is essential to use an acidic substrate, such as azalea soil, which can be mixed with gravel or clay granules for improved drainage. The plant may be cut back after the blooming period.

Propagation You can save top and side cuttings when pruning: they will take root in propagating soil under a plastic film cover; conditions should be moist and warm, around 25 °C (77 °F).

Cordyline terminalis

TI PLANT

Family Agaves (*Agavaceae*)

Origin This species originated in the Asian tropics and is still frequently identified by its former name, *C. fruticosa*. In its natural habitat it grows as a shrub; in our latitudes it will only grow as a houseplant. *C. australis* and *C. stricta* are hardier species that can live outdoors as container plants in the summer.

Characteristics With its colourful, lancet-shaped leaves, which can grow up to 50 cm (20 in) long, this bushy plant is definitely an eye-catcher. The main colour of the leaves is green, but depending upon the variety, they may have red, pink or yellowish stripes. The flowers are inconspicuous.

Location Ti plants prefer a bright location, but tolerate semi-shade (particularly the red-leafed varieties); avoid harsh midday sun. If the location is too dark, variegated plants become less strongly coloured. The temperature should never fall below 20°C (68 °F), and the relative humidity should be 60 per cent or more.

Watering and fertilising Ti plants require a substrate that is constantly moist; however, they will rot easily if standing water accumulates. Use only softened, room temperature water. Fertilise your plant once a week from spring until autumn; in winter, only once per month.

Care Depending on the size of the pot, re-pot the ti plant once a year or even less frequently; the best time is spring. If the plant loses too many leaves, you can cut it back; however, it will require temperatures around 30 °C (86 °F) to produce new growth.

Propagation Various methods are possible, but they may not always be successful for amateur gardeners. You can sow seeds in the springtime at 20 °C (68 °F), or take top and stem cuttings and cultivate them in an enclosed propagating case with a soil temperature of 25 °C (77 °F). Mossing is also possible. Pinch off the tops of young plants to encourage bushier growth.

Curcuma

TURMERIC

Family Gingers (*Zingiberaceae*)

Origin The *Curcuma* species are reed-like perennials that are native to tropical Asia and Australia. In recent years they have become a frequent addition to patio and houseplant assortments, sometimes going by the names ginger or plume.

Characteristics The turmeric rhizome produces thick tufts of elongated leaves. The flower stem – which can grow up to 50 cm

(20 in) long – bears a striking, cone-like inflorescence with sturdy pink spathes. The small, tube-shaped flowers are usually hidden inside. The leaves dry up in the autumn.

Turmeric is a popular spice in Indian cuisine. The rhizomes of certain species are processed for this purpose.

NOTE

Location Turmeric flourishes best in a warm, semi-shady location; the temperature should not fall below 18 °C (64 °F). If the plant is placed outdoors in summer it should be protected from rain and wind. This frost-sensitive species must be brought inside in the winter.

Watering and fertilising Water liberally during the growing period and fertilise once per month. Keep the plant nearly dry in the wintertime.

Care Turmeric requires a rest period in winter; keep it nearly dry and no warmer than 10–12 °C (50–54 °F). Re-pot it in the spring in good-quality potting soil.

Propagation Spring is the best time to propagate. You can divide larger plants and continue cultivating the sections in bright, moist conditions at about 18–20 °C (64–68 °F). Cuttings taken from young shoots may be cultivated under the same conditions. Seed propagation is also possible.

Cycas revoluta

SAGO PALM

Family Cycads (*Cycadaceae*)

Origin The sago palm is a native of Japan and South-east Asia. Thus, it is sometimes called the Japanese sago palm. It is also known as the king sago palm.

Characteristics The sago palm first develops a short, thick trunk. If the plant is given enough space, this trunk can reach heights of up to 3 m (10 ft); however, it grows very slowly. A frond-like tuft of large pinnae grows at its top, each one consisting of many small, leathery leaves. The individual leaf tips are quite sharp, and all parts of the plant are poisonous.

Location Bright to semi-shady; avoid blazing midday sun. The plant enjoys fresh air and may be placed in a protected location outdoors in the summer. It requires temperatures around 20 °C (68 °F) in summer, but prefers to be cooler in winter. Larger specimens require spacious surroundings.

Watering and fertilising Always keep the earth ball moderately moist during the growth period. In addition, supplement with low doses of fertiliser once a week; azalea or rhododendron fertiliser is recommended. The sago palm will not tolerate standing water, but it can survive longer dry periods quite well.

Care This cold-sensitive plant thrives at winter temperatures of 10–15 °C (50–59 °F). Keep the soil nearly dry during winter. In the spring it is important to accustom the palm to the strong outdoor sunlight gradually. You can re-pot the plant at this time if necessary, including a layer of clay granules under the sandy potting soil to improve drainage, but you need not do so every year.

Propagation Sow seeds in the springtime at 30 °C (86 °F); germination can take up to three months. You may well find that seeds are not very easily acquired.

! *Caution: Poisonous and/ or allergenic*

Cyclamen persicum

CYCLAMEN

Family Primroses *(Primulaceae)*

Origin The cyclamens we cultivate in our homes originally come from the eastern Mediterranean region. Many varieties have been developed from the wild species.

Characteristics The cyclamen's heart- or kidney-shaped, often patterned leaves are very decorative in and of themselves. They are further adorned by the distinctive, frequently fragrant flowers, which can be found in colours ranging from pink, red and

violet to white. Both large- and small-blossoming varieties are available, with simple, compound, fringed or wavy flowers. The plants may be as tall as 40 cm (15 in) or a compact 10 cm (4 in). Starting at summer's end, you can purchase blooming specimens throughout the winter.

Location Bright to semi-shady; avoid direct midday sun. Cyclamen prefers a cool room with temperatures of 12–15 °C (54–59 °F). In summer it can live outdoors in a semi-shady spot at temperatures up to 20 °C (68 °F). Be sure to keep humidity high.

Watering and fertilising Keep the substrate slightly moist, but avoid standing water. Always water the plant from below, via the planter or saucer. Fertilise once a week during the blooming period; then reduce fertiliser until the plant wilts.

Care A cyclamen can be cultivated for several years: just re-pot it every 1–2 years after the blooming period. Dig up the tuber, remove the old soil and re-plant, preferably in a clay pot. At least one-third of the tuber should protrude. Fertilise every 2 weeks until the plant blossoms.

Propagation Sow the dark-sprouting seeds in winter at ca. 18 °C (64 °F) and cover them with 2–3 cm of substrate. Prick out the seedlings after about 3 months; separate larger plants a second time. This job is best done by a professional gardener.

! *Caution: Poisonous and/or allergenic*

Cymbidium

CYMBIDIUM ORCHID

Family Orchids *(Orchidaceae)*

Origin Most of the nearly 50 species of *Cymbidium* are native to the tropics of South-east Asia, Japan and Australia. Our house-plants are hybrids cultivated from these species.

Characteristics Depending on the variety, these perennials can grow up to 50 cm (20 in) or more. The base of the shoots is thickened in the shape of a tuber. These pseudobulbs store water and nutrients. The slender, deep green leaves initially grow upright, then hang over in an arched shape. The striking flower clusters appear in the spring or summer; the colours vary from white or yellow to pink or red.

Location Place in a very bright and airy location that is warm in the summer (approx. 20–28 °C/68–82 °F) and cooler in winter (15–20 °C/59–68 °F). In midsummer, the orchid can even be placed on a balcony. The warm days and cool nights will automatically ensure that flowers develop. Otherwise, the plant requires three months of cooler temperatures – around 15 °C (59 °F). The humidity should never fall below 50 per cent.

Watering and fertilising Keep the substrate slightly moist at all times during the spring and summer. In winter, too, the plant should not be allowed to dry out. However, constant wetness will rot the roots. During the growing period, fertilise every two weeks at one-half concentration. Use only soft, room tempera-ture water.

Cymbidium orchid *Cymbidium*

Care Re-pot when the pot becomes too small. A good substrate may be made from part-peat potting soil mixed with orchid substrate and styromull. The pot should not be too large, or the plant will expend its energy forming leaves rather than blossoms.

Propagation You can separate pseudobulbs when re-potting and plant them individually.

Cyperus

CYPERUS

Family Sedges *(Cyperaceae)*

Origin *C. involucratus*, which originates in tropical Africa and South Africa, is the most common houseplant species. *C. papyrus* is the famous papyrus plant, which the Egyptians used for making paper.

Characteristics This bushy shrub can grow to heights of 1 m (3 ft) or more. An umbrella-shaped crown of delicate, slightly overhanging leaves forms at the ends of the reeds. From summer until autumn, these are joined by large umbels.

Location This plant likes bright conditions, but tolerates both sun and semi-shade. The location should be well ventilated and warm (approx. 30 °C/86 °F); the temperature should be cooler in winter but should not fall below 10 °C (50 °F). The cyperus will enjoy an outdoor location during the summer months – ideally beside a pond, if you have one. The humidity should be kept high at all times (around 70 per cent).

Watering and fertilising Cyperus is a marsh plant that needs to keep its feet constantly wet. Thus, you should make sure the planter or saucer remains filled with water. Hydroponic culture is highly recommended. You should mist the plant regularly, but not when it is standing in bright sunlight, since the leaves will become burnt. The cyperus should be fertilised every two weeks during the growing period, once a month in winter.

Care Re-pot the plant in part-clay soil and a plastic pot, since these materials retain water well.

Propagation Cyperus is very easy to propagate. Simply separate a leaf rosette, shorten the leaves slightly, and place it upside down in a glass of water. It will take root quickly and can then be planted in a pot. Large plants may be divided easily.

DAHLIA

Family Daisies, composite flowers (*Asteraceae*)

Origin Dahlias hail from Mexico. The numerous varieties we know today are the result of centuries of hybridisation.

Characteristics Bushy, compact miniature dahlias are ideal for a window or balcony box. Depending on the variety, they grow 15 to 30 cm (6–12 in) high and bloom in nearly every colour from spring until the first frost with simple or compound flowers.

Location Indoors, the location should be as bright as possible, but without direct sunlight. If you move the plants outdoors they will need to adjust to the stronger sunlight gradually.

Watering and fertilising Water regularly during the blooming period and fertilise once per week.

Care You can dig up the tubers in the autumn and store them in a dry, frost-free place until spring.

Propagation Smaller varieties of dahlias are often propagated via seeds in spring, at 18–20 °C (64–68 °F). Large tubers may be separated into sections with one axil apiece; plant in a nutrient-rich substrate and continue cultivating at the same temperature.

CHRYSANTHEMUM

Family Daisies, with composite flowers *(Asteraceae)*

Origin Japan, China. The varieties available for purchase may also be called *C. Indicum* or *C. Grandiflorum* hybrids.

Characteristics Thanks to the myriad types available, you can purchase this classic autumn flower in bloom almost year round, in nearly every colour, simple or compound, as a bush or a high-stemmed plant.

Location Bright, without direct sun; not too warm (approx. 18 °C/64 °F). If you wish to winter the plant over, keep it in a cool (5° C/41 °F) and bright location.

Watering and fertilising Keep moderately moist during the blooming period, but avoid standing water. Add fertiliser to the water every 2 weeks. Conditions should be drier in winter.

Care Chrysanthemums are generally seasonal, but if you wish to winter them over, re-pot them in a fresh substrate. Cut the plant back by two-thirds before the winter rest period.

Propagation Take cuttings from wintered-over plants in spring. Root them at ca. 18 °C (64 °F); new plants will bloom in autumn.

DENDROBIUM ORCHID

Family Orchids (*Orchidaceae*)

Origin The nearly 1400 species of *Dendrobium* are at home in Asia and the Pacific. Many hybrid forms are now available.

Characteristics The many species vary widely as far as the shape of the plants and flowers is concerned. Depending upon the variety, the elegant, often fragrant blossoms appear in the spring or summer. Dendrobiums are sympodial orchids. That means they produce new pseudobulbs every year, in which they store water and nutrients. Some species also lose their leaves after the blooming period.

Location The location should be bright in both summer and winter, but away from direct sunlight. Make sure the relative humidity is high, at least 60 per cent. Many species, such as *D. nobile*, are content at room temperature and may be placed outdoors in the summer. Others, such as *D. bigibbum*, will only flourish in a hothouse. It is best to enquire about each plant's specific needs before making a purchase.

Watering and fertilising Keep the substrate slightly moist during the vegetation period. Do not allow the plant to dry out; nor should standing water accumulate. Supplement the plant with a fertiliser at one-half concentration every two weeks during this period. If the pseudobulbs are firm and mature, you will need to water less. Use only softened, room temperature water. Mist the plant frequently when it is not in bloom.

Care Re-pot in special orchid substrate every two years in the spring. The roots should fill the pot well.

Propagation Sometimes a plant will produce offshoots, which may be separated along with their roots and re-planted. Alternatively, you can take stem cuttings containing one node each and lay them in a moist peat substrate; cover and cultivate under moist, warm conditions. New growth should appear after a few weeks.

DIEFFENBACHIA

Family Arum lilies (*Araceae*)

Origin This perennial's original habitat is the West Indies; it is also commonly known by its alternative name, *D. maculata*. A wide variety of types are available.

Characteristics The dieffenbachia may grow in a bushy pattern or develop a thick trunk. It is greatly admired for its large, distinctive, white or yellow variegated leaves. The leaf shapes and colours vary widely depending upon the type. One well known variety is 'Tropic Snow', whose broad, dark green leaves

are speckled with greenish yellow. When dieffenbachia blooms, a spadix appears surrounded by a green or white spathe.

Location Bright to semi-shady, without direct sunlight. Temperatures should be at least 20 °C (68 °F) throughout the year, with around 60 per cent relative humidity. Avoid draughts.

Watering and fertilising Keep the soil moist at all times, but do not allow standing water to accumulate or the roots will rot. The water should be as low in lime as possible; hydroponic culture works well for this plant. Water somewhat less in winter. Fertilise once a week from spring until autumn; every 2–3 weeks during the winter months.

Care You can re-pot dieffenbachia any time from spring until autumn as necessary – usually every two years. A plant that has become bare may be cut back and will develop strong new growth. When cut, the plant emits a juice that can irritate the skin, so it is best to wear gloves when working with it, and do not put any parts of the plant in your mouth.

Propagation Top cuttings or stem cuttings require high humidity and temperatures of 22–24 °C (72–75 °F) in order to develop roots and new growth. You can initially root top cuttings in a glass of water. Poke the stem cuttings diagonally into the substrate like dibbles.

! *Caution: Poisonous and/or allergenic*

Dracaena marginata

DRACAENA

Family Dracaenas _(Dracaenaceae)_

Origin This species originally comes from Reunion Island in the Indian Ocean. Another well known species is _D. fragrans_, which bears a tuft of wide, yellow and green striped leaves on its sturdy trunk. _D. deremensis_ is very popular as well; it is completely covered with shiny green, white or yellow striped leaves.

Characteristics _Dracaena marginata_ has a tuft of long, narrow leaves at the end of its slender trunk; they are dark green on the surface and reddish underneath. Thus, it is also known as a bordered dragon tree or ribbon plant.

Location Bright to semi-shady, but not direct sunlight. The leaf pattern is less pronounced if the plant does not get enough light. Temperatures should be ca. 20 °C (68 °F) in summer, or 15 °C (59 °F) in winter. Aim for a relative humidity of 50 per cent.

TIP
If the air is too dry, spider mites, scale insects or thrips may infest the plant.

Watering and fertilising Keep the earth ball only slightly moist; water less in the winter or if the location is dark. Fertilise weekly from spring until autumn.

Care It is sufficient to re-pot your dracaena in fresh substrate every 2–3 years. Wipe the sturdy leaves occasionally with a damp cloth.

140

Propagation Top or stem cuttings will produce new plants most quickly. It is best to take them in the spring or summer and plant them in a propagating substrate; cultivate under plastic film in a bright location at 25 °C (77 °F). Nurseries frequently offer stem sections that are already partially rooted.

Echinocactus grusonii

GOLDEN BARREL CACTUS

Family Cacti (*Cactaceae*)

Origin Mother-in-law's seat – as this species is sometimes cheekily called because of its shape and sharp thorns – has its natural home in the hot desert regions of Mexico.

Characteristics The golden barrel cactus has a broad, spherical shape; older specimens may have up to 30 ribs, all studded with sharp, yellow thorns. Grown outdoors, it can reach almost

Golden barrel cactus *Echinocactus grusonii*

1m (3 ft) in height and 1 m in diameter; however, it grows extremely slowly. In summer older cacti may develop bell-shaped flowers in the upper central region or crown; these are brown on the outside and yellow inside.

Location The cactus requires sunny, warm and dry conditions. It should receive at least five to six hours of full sun during the day. In midsummer, at temperatures of 25 °C (77 °F) or higher, the cactus can stand outdoors. In winter the daytime temperature should be 18–20 °C (64–68 °F) and should not drop below 10 °C (50 °F) at night; otherwise the plant will quickly rot.

Watering and fertilising During the growing period, water only if the substrate is dry. Add a cactus fertiliser to the water every two weeks. Do not water or fertilise in winter.

Care If the cactus's pot becomes too small, it is time to re-pot. The substrate should be as porous as possible – that is, sandy or gravely. The best choice is a special cactus soil.

Propagation From spring until early summer, you can sow seeds in a sandy propagating soil or directly into cactus substrate. Mist the seeds, cover with clear plastic film and place them in a bright and warm location (at least 20 °C/68 °F). The slow-growing young plants will need to be pricked out several times. Successful seed propagation is not always easy.

Epiphyllum hybrids
ORCHID CACTUS

Family Cacti (*Cactaceae*)

Origin The original species from which our houseplants are descended are at home in South America and Mexico. The numerous hybrids are the result of crosses between various species.

Characteristics The orchid cactus forms angular shoots which grow 80–90 cm (31–36 in) long. It is extremely popular, thanks in part to its large, funnel-shaped and often fragrant flowers. Orchid cacti can be found in many colours; depending upon the variety they may be red, pink, purple, yellowish or white. The main blooming period is in the summer; a second round of flowers may appear in autumn or winter. Red fruits develop after the blooming period.

Location Very bright, but avoid the blazing sun. An airy, shady location on a balcony or patio is ideal in the summertime. The plant will do well under warm daytime conditions (20–25 °C/ 68–77 °F) during the warmer months; it should be somewhat cooler at night. In the winter, this frost-sensitive cactus prefers temperatures around 10 °C (50 °F); it is happy to live in a rather cool room.

Watering and fertilising Since this succulent plant is very sensitive to lime, water only with soft water. Keep the substrate slightly moist from spring until autumn and supplement with cactus fertiliser every four weeks. Water only sparingly in winter.

Care Re-pot in the springtime in fresh, sandy soil with a low pH value, or in special cactus substrate. It is not necessary to re-pot every year.

Propagation You can take cuttings from mature shoots in the late spring or in the summertime. Allow the cuttings to dry out before sticking them in dry sand, where they will take root. Do not water the new plants until three weeks after roots have formed.

Epipremnum pinnatum

POTHOS

Family Arum lilies *(Araceae)*

Origin The speckled-leaf species, which is also known as devil's ivy or centipede Tonga vine, is a native of the Pacific island region. It is closely related to *E. aureum* or golden pothos. In their natural habitat, both species grow as shrubs. They are truly classics among our houseplants.

Characteristics This evergreen plant forms shoots several metres long, which may be allowed to hang down or secured to

a trellis. Its leathery, heart-shaped leaves are a fresh green with an irregular yellow pattern; the 'Silver Queen' variety has a whitish-yellow leaf pattern. In older plants, the leaves are deeply grooved and may grow up to 50 cm (20 in) long.

Location Bright to semi-shady, away from the blazing sun. The darker the plant's location, however, the less pronounced the leaf patterns will be. Temperatures should remain consistent throughout the year, at a minimum of 20 °C (68 °F), with a relative humidity of 60 per cent or more. The pothos will also tolerate somewhat lower temperatures in the winter.

Watering and fertilising Keep the earth ball slightly moist at all times during the growing period, and somewhat drier in the winter. The amount of water required depends upon the plant's location and size. Take care that the substrate does not dry out; hydroponic culture is a good solution. The pothos requires a dose of fertiliser every 1–2 weeks from spring until autumn; every 3–4 weeks is sufficient the rest of the year.

Care Younger plants should be re-potted every year in fresh, nutrient-rich potting soil. Older specimens in large pots may be re-potted less often.

Propagation You can make top or section cuttings in spring, which will root in a glass of water or in moist propagating soil covered with plastic film at 25 °C (77 °F).

Erica
HEATH

Family Heathers (*Ericaceae*)

Origin Most of the nearly 800 *Erica* species originated in South Africa – Cape heath (*E. gracilis*) is one example. Winter heath (*E. carnea*) and bell heather (*E. cinerea*) also grow in Europe.

Characteristics These bushy, evergreen shrubs with needle-like leaves usually grow between 20 and 50 cm (8–20 in) high. During the blooming period, they produce a multitude of small, bell-shaped flowers. Cape heath, with its fragrant clusters of white, pink or red blossoms, is a typical plant for an autumn balcony. Winter heath will bloom through the winter until spring; bell heather blooms from summer to autumn with white, pink, purple or red flowers, depending on the variety. These heaths may be planted in the garden after the blooming period.

Location Sunny; *E. gracilis* can also stand in a semi-shady spot.

Watering and fertilising Heathers prefer a moist substrate, but won't tolerate standing water. Since they only flourish in low-lime, acidic soil, it is best to use softened water or rainwater.

Care Cape heath is not winter-hardy and is usually not culti-vated past the blooming period. The perennial varieties need to be pruned back after the flowering period so they can produce new bushy growth and bloom in the next season. Be careful not to cut too deep into the older wood of the plant. Winter heath can tolerate frost, but bell heather appreciates shelter in winter.

Propagation Take semi-mature cuttings from non-blooming side branches in late summer and autumn. They should be ca. 5 cm (2 in) long and include uniformly sized, thickly growing leaves. Root them at 15–20 °C (59–68 °F), airing the young plants daily. Treat prophylactically with a fungicide to prevent rotting moulds. Pinch off the young plants' tops several times.

Euphorbia pulcherrima

POINSETTIA

Family Spurges *(Euphorbiaceae)*

Origin The genus *Euphorbia* includes approximately 2,000 species. The poinsettia – also known as the Christmas flower or Christmas star – originally comes from the southern part of Mexico and Central America, where it grows as a shrub, to impressive heights of up to 3 m (10 ft).

Characteristics Poinsettias sold as houseplants most often stand 20–30 cm (8–12 in) tall; however, miniature and long-stemmed forms are also available. The inconspicuous, yellowish

green flowers are surrounded by large, striking spathes. These can now be found in many colours, ranging from red, pink, salmon-coloured and white to bicoloured varieties.

Location As bright as possible, but avoid harsh sunlight. A warm location (at least 18 °C/64 °F) is ideal. This plant does not appreciate dry, artificially heated air or draughts.

Watering and fertilising Keep the substrate uniformly moist, but do not allow standing water to build up. Use only room temperature water. If you keep the poinsettia beyond the Christmas season, it should be fertilised every week from spring until autumn; in winter only every two weeks.

Care If you wish to keep your poinsettia after the holiday season, it is best to prune it back radically in the spring or summer and re-pot it. If you want it to bloom again at Christmastime, it must be kept in a dark place for at least 12 hours per day for a period of six weeks in the autumn.

Propagation Poinsettias may be cultivated from top cuttings, but it is not particularly easy. Since the plant releases a poisonous, milky sap, work cautiously. It is important to place the cut edges in lukewarm water before planting them to allow the sap to drain out. Afterwards, keep the cuttings in a bright, sunny location (25–30 °C/77–86 °F).

■ *Caution: Poisonous and/or allergenic*

Eustoma grandiflorum

LISIANTHUS

Family Gentians *(Gentianaceae)*

Origin The large-flowered prairie gentian or Texas bluebell is native to the northern and south-eastern United States, Colorado and northern Mexico.

Characteristics The bell-shaped flowers appear in the summer; they may be blue, pink, violet or white and simple or compound in form. Lisianthus is available as a bushy, compact potted plant for the house or patio, or as a long-stemmed and long-lasting cut flower. Its fleshy leaves are greyish green.

Location Very bright, but avoid harsh sunlight. Outdoors, the plant's location should be protected from wind and rain. Keep it at 8–12 °C (46–54 °F) in the wintertime.

Watering and fertilising During the vegetation period, water the plant just enough to avoid both dryness and standing water; fertilise every 2–3 weeks. Water only sparingly in winter.

Care Since the Lisianthus is an annual plant, there is no need to re-pot it.

Propagation To cultivate the plant as a biennial, sow seeds in late summer; for annual cultivation, in February or March – in both cases, at temperatures of 20–25 °C (70–77 °F). Continue cultivating the pricked-out young plants at 15–18 °C (59–64 °F). A sandy, porous substrate is very important.

Exacum affine
PERSIAN VIOLET

Family Gentians *(Gentianaceae)*

Origin Socotra Island in the Gulf of Aden.

Characteristics This bushy, compact plant grows up to 30 cm (12 in) high. Its fleshy, abundantly branching stems are entirely covered with leaves. The small, fragrant flowers appear without a pause from early summer until autumn; they can be found in various shade of blue as well as violet and white.

Location Bright to semi-shady; protect the plant from the harsh midday sun. Keep the Persian violet at temperatures between 18 and 25 °C (64–77 °F) indoors; somewhat cooler in the winter (approximately 15 °C/59 °F). This plant can also spend the summer on a balcony.

Watering and fertilising Keep the earth ball slightly moist at all times and fertilise once a week from spring until autumn.

Care The Persian violet is not usually cultivated beyond the blooming period.

Propagation This plant can be cultivated as an annual or as a biennial. Thus, you can sow seeds from winter until spring at 20–22 °C (68–72 °F). Cover them with glass or plastic film (they are light-germinating). Alternatively, take cuttings in springtime.

x Fatshedera lizei
ARALIA IVY

Family Aralias *(Araliaceae)*

Origin This cultivated species was developed in 1912 at the French tree nursery of Lize-Freres, from a cross between a Japanese aralia *(Fatsia japonica)* and an ivy *(Hedera helix)*.

Characteristics Depending upon its location, this evergreen, shrub-like plant can grow several metres high. It grows upright and by nature, branches very little. Its leathery, three-lobed leaves are very decorative. In addition to the green variety, 'Variegata', with white-edged leaves is also available; the 'Silver Prince' variety has a silver-grey hue.

Location The aralia ivy can live in bright, semi-shady or shady locations; however, the coloured-leaf varieties require more light than the green types. It is an ideal plant for cool to moderately warm rooms; during its winter rest period, it is content at temperatures around 10 °C (50 °F). It can be moved to a patio or balcony during the summer months. Mist the leaves frequently.

Watering and fertilising Keep the earth ball slightly moist from spring until early autumn; take care that it does not dry out. Add a dose of fertiliser to the water once per week. The plant takes a rest period in the winter and requires only minimal watering.

Care Aralia ivy is extremely hardy and easy to care for. Nevertheless, you should re-pot it in the spring in good, nutrient-rich soil, preferably in a plastic pot.

Propagation Take top or stem cuttings at any time of year. They will grow quickly at air and soil temperatures of 20–25 °C (77 °F). The ideal cuttings are semi-mature, already firm at the base but still growing at the tips. A rooting medium is helpful, particularly if the cuttings are already woody.

Fatsia japonica

FATSIA

Family Aralias *(Araliaceae)*

Origin This species, also called Japanese aralia, is a native of the Riukiu Islands of Japan and of South Korea, where it grows in the brushwood to heights of up to 4 m (13 ft).

Characteristics The fatsia's shiny, leathery leaves, with deep, multiple lobes, are its most eye-catching feature. In this species they are dark green; the 'Variegata' variety has leaves with white or yellow colouring. The cultivated forms of fatsia grow much more slowly than it does in nature.

Location The ideal location is bright to semi-shady; fatsia does not like direct sunlight. It will also tolerate a shady spot, but its growth will not be as lush. It prefers a cool to moderately warm room, with temperatures between 10 and 20 °C (50–68 °F). Container plants are happy to stand outdoors in the summer. They will even tolerate light frost, but are best wintered over under bright conditions at 5–10 °C (41–50 °F).

Watering and fertilising The substrate needs to be kept moist at all times from spring until autumn, but do not allow standing water to accumulate. It is better to water twice a day if necessary. You should also fertilise the fatsia once a week during this period. Water less in winter, but even then the soil should not dry out completely. The more frequently the leaves are misted, the more beautifully they will develop.

Care This undemanding plant normally needs re-potting only every 2–4 years, especially if it is planted in a large container. The best time to re-pot is in early spring, before the plant begins producing new growth. Larger specimens may be cut back significantly.

Propagation You can sow seeds from late winter until spring, or propagate via top or section cuttings in the springtime. The best temperature for propagation is 20 °C (68 °F).

! *Caution: Poisonous and/or allergenic*

Ficus benjamina
WEEPING FIG

Family Mulberries *(Moraceae)*

Origin The well known weeping fig, which is also known under the name Benjamin fig, is at home from the Himalayas and India all the way to northern Australia. The widely varied *Ficus* genus comprises nearly 800 species.

Characteristics This evergreen indoor tree grows upright with slightly overhanging branches. Its leathery leaves are elliptical in shape and pointed at the ends. You can choose between a wide range of types: solid green, green and white, yellowish green or even tricoloured patterns, with flat or wavy leaves.
Caution: The weeping fig contains a milky sap.

TIP

The selection of Ficus species available is vast. Here are a few more of the most familiar houseplants:
• F. binnendijkii, with long, narrow, dark green leaves
• F. cyathistipula, with dark green leaves 10–25 cm (4–10 in) long; produces abundant fruit
• F. deltoidea, the mistletoe fig, compact and slow growing, with spatula shaped leaves and small, round fruits
• F. lyrata, fiddle leaf fig or banjo fig, with violin-shaped leaves up to 30 cm (12 in) long; also well suited to shady locations
• F. pumila, creeping fig, with thin branches bearing delicate, egg shaped green or white variegated leaves; well suited for hanging baskets or ground cover

• F. sagittata, *hanging branches with arrow shaped, pointed leaves; either solid green or green and white variegated; for hanging baskets or ground cover*

Location Bright, but protected from the blazing midday sun. A consistent soil temperature of around 20 °C (68 °F) is important. The air temperature should not fall below 18 °C (64 °F), even in winter. Keep the relative humidity high – at least 50 per cent. If exposed to draughts or moved frequently, the plant will often lose its leaves.

Weeping fig *Ficus benjamina*

Watering and fertilising The earth ball should be kept slightly moist at all times. However, if the plant is too wet, it will drop its leaves. It is best to always feel the soil with your fingers to see how moist it is before adding water. Weeping figs flourish beautifully in hydroponic culture and appreciate frequent misting. Fertilise every one or two weeks from spring until autumn; the rest of the year, every six weeks.

NOTE

*If the surrounding air is too dry,
spider mites can often be a problem.*

Care Younger plants in smaller pots should be re-planted every year, older ones every 2–3 years in ordinary potting soil.

Propagation Cuttings from young but mature shoots require high air and soil temperatures (ca. 25–30 °C/77–86 °F) as well as high humidity (ca. 70 per cent) in order to develop roots. Propagation is most successful during the summer months under a plastic film cover. Allow the cut edges to dry before planting the cuttings. Alternatively, you can produce new plants via mossing (see page 36). Keep in mind that the plant releases a sticky, milky sap when cut, which may irritate your skin or leave stains on fabric.

! *Caution: Poisonous and/or allergenic*

162

Ficus elastica

RUBBER TREE

Family Mulberries *(Moraceae)*

Origin Eastern Himalaya, Indonesia

Characteristics This tree, single-stemmed in nature, can stand several metres even in a container. Its broad, oval, leathery leaves, up to 40 cm (15 in) long, are dark green in the main species. Depending on the variety, they may also have yellow, white or grey patterns.

Location Bright, but out of direct midday sun. Rubber trees tolerate a temperature range of 15 to 30 °C (59–86 °F), but drastic temperature changes should be avoided. This tropical plant requires high humidity.

Watering and fertilising Water regularly, preferably with lukewarm water. Allow the substrate to dry out between waterings. Fertilise once a week from spring until autumn.

Care Cut back overly long or unattractively shaped plants; the trimmed plant will need a bright and warm spot to encourage new growth. Otherwise, care is the same as for the weeping fig.

Propagation In the spring or summer via mossing.

❗ *Caution: Poisonous and/or allergenic*

163

FUCHSIA

Family Nightshades (*Onagraceae*)

Origin In their homeland of South America, fuchsias are found as semi-shrubs, small trees and even climbing plants. Intensive cultivation has resulted in a vast assortment of types.

Characteristics Depending on the variety, fuchsias may grow upright or overhanging, and can reach heights up to 1 m (3 ft). The generally overhanging flowers each consist of four sepals and four petals. The sepals and petals may be the same colour, but are frequently contrasting. The simple or compound flowers grow in clusters or panicles. The blooming period extends from spring until autumn. The fuchsia's oval-shaped leaves are usually green, but variegated types have been developed in recent years.

Location Semi-shady to shady, protected from wind and rain. Sun-tolerant varieties exist now as well; these do not take a rest from blooming in midsummer.

Watering and fertilising Fuchsia will tolerate neither dry soil nor standing water; thus, you should water uniformly. On hot, dry days, you can even give the leaves an additional shower. Fuchsia has a high nutrient requirement during the growth period. Since the plants are sensitive to salt, it is better to fertilise frequently but in low doses.

Care Remove wilted flowers and seed stems regularly. Fuchsias are frost-sensitive and are best kept indoors in the winter. They

164

can also be wintered over in the dark, provided you keep the temperature lower than 10 °C (50 °F) and water very sparingly. Cut the plants back in the spring and re-pot if necessary.

Propagation You can take top cuttings at any time of year; however, the best time is in spring when you prune the plant back. They will take root most rapidly at around 20 °C (68 °F).

Gardenia augusta

GARDENIA

Family Madders *(Rubiaceae)*

Origin Japan, the Riukiu Islands, Taiwan and China are the native homes of this elegant shrub, which is still frequently known by its former name, *G. jasminoides*.

Characteristics Gardenias grow around 30 cm (12 in) high as potted plants; in containers they may reach an imposing 1.5 m (5 ft). This evergreen shrub is charming all year round with its shiny, dark green leaves, but the real highlight is the large, fragrant, pure white flowers that appear from July through October. Depending upon the variety, they may be simple or compound.

NOTE

If your gardenia drops its buds, its location may be too dark or too warm during the budding and flowering period. It will have the same reaction to excessive dryness or frequent changes in location.

Location Very bright, but without direct sunlight. From spring until autumn, the plant will flourish at consistent air and soil temperatures of 18 to 25 °C (64–77 °F), with high humidity. During the winter rest period, it prefers to be cool – approximately 10–15 °C (50–59 °F). In warm summer weather, the plant can also stand outdoors.

Watering and fertilising Water moderately throughout the summer and mist frequently. In winter, water just enough that the soil doesn't dry out, using lime-free water only. During the growing period, supplement every two weeks with an acidifying fertiliser – e. g. azalea fertiliser – at one-half concentration.

Care Re-pot every one or two years in the late winter, using a low-pH substrate. Mix the soil with expanded clay for better drainage. You can give the plant a thinning or shaping trim at this time, if necessary.

Propagation In the summer, root top cuttings in a mixture of sand and peat under plastic film at 25 °C (77 °F). Pinch off the tops of the young plants several times.

Genista x spachiana
EASTER BROOM

Family Peas *(Fabaceae)*

Origin Easter broom, or Canary broom after its native home in the Canary Islands, where the shrub grows up to 2 m (7 ft) high, is also sold under its former Latin name, *Cytisus x racemosus*.

Characteristics This bushy species is available as a houseplant or as a container plant, and may grow up to 1 m (3 ft) high with proper care. It owes its popularity to its gleaming yellow, fragrant blossoms, which appear in long clusters in early spring – even as early as January, depending on the location. They form a striking contrast to the dark green, three-part leaves.

Location Sunny, bright and airy; an ideal plant for cooler rooms or stairwells. In summer the Easter broom prefers a spot on the balcony or patio to the living room. It needs to come back indoors in autumn, where it should be kept in a bright spot at around 10 °C (50 °F) over the winter. If the winter temperature is too warm, the plant will bloom poorly the following spring.

Watering and fertilising During the vegetation period, from spring until autumn, keep the soil moist at all times. This plant requires a weekly dose of fertiliser during this time. Water significantly less in the winter.

Care If you cut your Easter broom back by one-third to one-half after the blooming period it will grow back bushier than ever. Re-pot in fresh soil every 1–2 years as necessary in spring.

Easter broom *Genista x spachiana*

Propagation Semi-mature cuttings taken in the summer will grow quickly at 18–20 °C (64–68 °F). It is helpful to add a rooting hormone. The parent plant should be an abundant bloomer; cuttings from the top of the plant are preferable to side cuttings. Prop the young plants several times.

! *Caution: Poisonous and/or allergenic*

Gerbera jamesonii

GERBERA

Family Daisies, composite flowers (*Asteraceae*)

Origin South Africa. Hybridisation has produced myriad varieties of this perennial.

Characteristics Gerbera is very popular as a cut flower, and in recent years has become increasingly available on the market as a compact potted plant. It forms thick leaf rosettes and may grow between 20 and 60 cm (8–24 in) tall. The large flowers are extremely long-lasting. They can be found in a multitude of colours, from red and pink to orange and yellow to white, simple or compound. Gerbera blooms throughout the year.

Location Very bright to sunny. Consistent temperatures around 20 °C (68 °F) are recommended in summer. Under these conditions, the gerbera is happy to spend the warm months outdoors. It needs to come inside before the first frost. Its location can be somewhat cooler in winter – around 15–18 °C (59–64 °F) – but the earth ball shouldn't become chilled (i.e. on a cold windowsill). Flowers will only develop in temperatures above 12 °C (54 °F).

Watering and fertilising The substrate should be moderately moist; it should not be allowed to dry out, nor should standing water accumulate. This flowering plant requires a weekly dose of fertiliser from spring until autumn.

Care Remove a few leaves to help the plant receive more light in the winter. Re-pot in the early spring, in sandy, nutrient-rich soil. Since the gerbera has a very long taproot, be sure to select a sufficiently large container.

Check your plants carefully and regularly for evidence of white flies and aphids.

TIP

Propagation Larger plants may be divided. Seed propagation is possible in the spring or autumn. Cover the seeds with newspaper and keep them at temperatures of 21–24 °C (70–75 °F). Continue cultivating the young plants at 18–20 °C (64–68°F).

Glechoma hederacea

GROUND IVY

Family Labiates or mints (*Lamiaceae*)

Origin Also called creeping Charlie, cat-foot or Gill-over-the-ground; native to Europe.

Characteristics This perennial can grow as a hanging plant or creeper, quickly forming a thick carpet. 'Variegata' is a widespread variety with rounded green and white leaves that release an intense fragrance when touched. The whorled flower axes with blue-violet blossoms appear from early summer.

Location Bright to semi-shady, indoors and out. Ideal temperatures are 18–20 °C (64–68 °F) in summer; slightly cooler in winter.

Watering and fertilising Soil should be quite moist at all times. If the substrate dries out, the leaves turn brown. Fertilise every two weeks in the growth period; every two months in winter at half concentration. Water significantly less in winter.

Care To cultivate ground ivy for several years, re-pot as needed in nutrient-rich, sandy soil, cutting the plant back beforehand. To be on the safe side, keep the plant frost-free over the winter.

Propagation Runners root easily at the nodes, at ca. 20 °C (68 °F).

 Caution: Poisonous and/or allergenic

HEBE

Family Figworts (*Scrophulariaceae*)

Origin Hybrids of various species.

Characteristics This little shrub's leathery green, white, or yellow variegated leaves are just as attractive as its large clusters of flowers, which appear in late summer to autumn in shocks of violet, blue, red, pink or white.

Location Bright to sunny, but avoid harsh midday sun; green-leafed varieties also tolerate semi-shade. Well suited to balconies, patios or cooler rooms (12–18 °C/54–64 °F). In regions with mild winters hebe can remain outdoors in winter; otherwise, move to a bright, cool room (5–10 °C/41–50 °F) after the blooming period.

Watering and fertilising Keep the earth ball moist during the warm season; drier in winter. Fertilise every two weeks during the growing period; every 4–6 weeks for the rest of the year.

Care Re-pot every one to two years in the springtime. You can prune the plant back in the spring or after the blooming period.

Propagation Take top cuttings in spring and root at soil temperatures of 15–20 °C (59–68 °F). Pinch off the tops several times.

173

Ivy

Family Aralias *(Araliaceae)*

Origin Common or English ivy is native to Europe.

Characteristics This evergreen climbing plant can creep up walls or along the ground for up to 10 m (33 ft) in nature; as a houseplant, it remains quite a bit smaller. Its decorative leaves are usually triangular in shape. Depending on the variety, they may have three to five lobes and be either flat or curly. They may be solid green, or have various patterns of green and white or green and yellow. *H. canariensis* 'Gloire de Marengo' has large green and white leaves and tolerates warm temperatures well. For outdoor planting, inquire about frost-hardy varieties.

NOTE *Ingesting any part of this plant will cause severe nausea.*

Location Green-leafed varieties do best in a semi-shady to shady location; those with variegated leaves prefer bright to semi-shady conditions, but without direct sunlight. From spring until autumn, temperatures of 18–20 °C (64–68 °F) are ideal; 10–15 °C (50–59 °F) is sufficient in the winter months.

Watering and fertilising Keep the soil moderately moist at all times; do not allow it to dry out. Mist the plant frequently, since spider mites can infest it quickly if the air is too dry. The darker the ivy's location, the less water it will need. If the substrate is too wet, the plant will rot easily. Fertilise once a week from spring until autumn.

Care Treat your ivy to a fresh substrate every year. You can give the plant a shaping trim at any time.

Propagation Cultivate tender cuttings in spring at 18–20 °C (64–68 °F). Alternatively, secure a shoot in a pot of flower soil, allow it to root and then separate it from the parent plant.

Helianthus annuus

SUNFLOWER

Family Daisies, composite flowers (*Asteraceae*)

Origin The common sunflower originally comes from the western United States and has been naturalised into Europe.

Characteristics Tall varieties grow quickly to heights of up to 3 m (10 ft); compact varieties for pots or balcony boxes remain much smaller, 30–80 cm (12–31 in). Both types are known for the large flowerheads they sport throughout the summer. The centre, made up of mostly brown disk flowers, is surrounded by yellow, reddish, brown, white or bicoloured florets.

NOTE *Touching the leaves of the sunflower may spark an allergic reaction in sensitive people.*

Location Sunny; place tall varieties in a wind-protected location.

Watering and fertilising Water liberally during the blooming period and fertilise once per week.

Care This annual plant flourishes best in a nutrient-rich, porous substrate.

Propagation Sow seeds at the end of winter or in early spring, either indoors or directly in their intended location.

HELIOTROPE

Family Borages and forget-me-nots (*Boraginaceae*)

Origin This evergreen semi-shrub is native to Peru.

Characteristics This plant, which grows between 30 and 60 cm (12–24 in) high, may be cultivated either as a bush or as a long-stemmed plant. It is characterised by the large, vanilla-scented umbels it produces without interruption until well into autumn. Both violet and blue varieties are available; both colours create an attractive contrast to the longish, corrugated, dark green leaves. The heliotrope contains poisonous alkaloids.

Location Sunny, warm, protected from wind and rain.

Watering and fertilising Water generously in the growth period, avoiding both standing water and dryness. Fertilise weekly.

Care This frost-sensitive plant is frequently kept for only one season. However, you can winter it over quite successfully in a bright, well ventilated room at temperatures of 5–10 °C (41–50 °F); water only sparingly. Re-pot the plant in a nutrient-rich substrate in the spring and prune it back.

Propagation Sow seeds at 18 °C (64 °F) in early spring, or take cuttings in summer. Pinch the tops of young plants frequently.

! *Caution: Poisonous and/or allergenic*

HELLEBORE

Family Buttercups *(Ranunculaceae)*

Origin The 15 species of this genus originally come from the forest regions of Europe and western Asia.

Characteristics These distinctive perennials are among the few plants which begin blooming in the winter. One of the best-known species is the Christmas rose, *Helleborus niger*, whose cup-shaped white flowers appear starting in December. They are frequently available during the Christmas season as potted plants for the house or patio. In addition to the pure species, there are numerous hybrids, most of which bloom in the early spring. Depending upon the variety, the colours range from purplish-red to yellow to white. The 'spotted hybrids' have petals that are speckled on the inside. The plants grow between 20 and 40 cm high and have dark green, deeply lobed, leathery leaves all year round. All parts of the plant are poisonous, particularly the seeds. The plant's sap can be irritating to the skin.

Location A cool, semi-shady to shady location. Potted plants do best if planted in the garden after the blooming period. Although the hybrids are generally very robust and frost-hardy, in colder regions they should be covered lightly until they begin to bloom.

Watering and fertilising Whether the plant is potted or in the garden, the substrate should always be kept well moistened. *H. niger* may be kept somewhat drier.

178

Care Over the long term, hellebores will only flourish well in nutrient-rich, humus soil.

Propagation After the blooming period, you can divide the plant or sow freshly harvested seeds. In order to wake them from dormancy, you must expose the seeds to the cold of winter. Hellebores also sow their own seeds easily. You can also re-plant the tiny seedlings that sprout up around the parent plant.

! *Caution: Poisonous and/or allergenic*

HIBISCUS

Family Mallows (*Malvaceae*)

Origin The Chinese hibiscus or rose of China, as this shrub is also called, originally comes from tropical Asia.

Characteristics Container plants may grow up to 3 m (10 ft) tall; potted houseplants grow to a maximum of 1 m (3 ft). You can cultivate them in a bushy or long-stemmed shape. From spring until autumn they produce large, eye-catching, funnel-

shaped flowers that – depending on the variety – may be simple or compound in the colours red, pink, orange, yellow or white. They form a lovely contrast to the plant's shiny dark green leaves.

Location Hibiscus needs the brightest spot possible to blossom abundantly, but do protect it from the blazing midday sun. It requires warm conditions (20 °C/68 °F or warmer); in winter, 14–20 °C (57–68 °F) is sufficient. Keep the humidity high.

If the flowers fall off, dry air or a change of location may be the cause.

TIP

Watering and fertilising During the blooming period, the hibiscus requires large amounts of water and nutrients. The water should permeate the soil, but do not allow standing water to build up. Fertilise the plant once a week and mist it frequently, using only lime-free water. Water the plant less in the winter and fertilise only once every 2–3 weeks.

Care Re-pot small plants every spring; larger ones every two years. Thin the branches if necessary, or cut the shoots back by one-third.

Propagation From spring to summer, you can take top cuttings from mature but non-woody shoots and root them under plastic film at air and soil temperatures of 20–25 °C (68–77 °F). Place them in a warm location; add a rooting medium if necessary. Pinch the tops of the young plants frequently.

Hippeastrum hybrids
AMARYLLIS

Family Amaryllis (*Amaryllidaceae*)

Origin The many varieties of amaryllis are the result of hybridisations between various species native to South America.

Characteristics Although *Hippeastrum* is well known by the common name amaryllis, it is not to be confused with the "true" amaryllis, *Amaryllis bella-donna* or belladonna lily. The plant's large bulb first produces long, strap-like leaves. The up to 60-cm (2-ft)-long flower stalk appears in autumn; it bears several large star-shaped blossoms. The plant's height is dependent upon the variety, as is the colour of the flowers: they may be red, pink, yellow, white or multi-coloured.

Location Sunny and bright. During the growing period until the leaves recede in September-October, keep the plant at temperatures of 20–22 °C (68–72 °F). Amaryllis requires a cool period at 13–16 °C (55–61 °F) of about six weeks, from October until new growth appears, in order to stimulate blooming. During the warm summer months, the amaryllis can live outdoors. It is very sensitive to frost.

Watering and fertilising Shortly before flowers begin to form, and during the blooming period, keep the substrate slightly moist. Gradually reduce watering when the leaves wilt, and begin again as new growth appears. After the blooming period, fertilise weekly until August. Cut off the flower stalk after the blooming period.

Care Re-pot at the end of the rest period. The new pot should be only a few centimetres larger than the bulb, one-third of which should protrude from the soil. It is best to loosen the substrate by mixing it with sand and to add an organic or time-release fertiliser.

Propagation Separate any bulblets which have formed roots and re-pot them. It is also possible to sow seeds, but you will be rewarded with blooming plants only three to four years later.

HYDRANGEA

Family Hydrangeas *(Hydrangeaceae)*

Origin The garden hydrangea is native to Japan and Korea; it has been cultivated in Europe since the eighteenth century.

Characteristics This deciduous shrub may reach 1.5 m (5 ft) in a container; potted plants remain much smaller (30–40 cm/ 12–15 in). The ball-shaped inflorescences appear in midsummer and may be blue, red, pink or white, depending on the variety. Lace-cap hydrangeas have flat flower axes surrounded by petals

only at the edges. Pre-cultivated plants are already available in the springtime. The hydrangea's leaves are large with a broad oval shape and serrated edges. They may cause skin irritation.

Location Bright to semi-shady, but out of direct midday sun. It should not be kept too warm indoors (maximum 20 °C/68 °F); it can stand outside in summer. Bring a hydrangea indoors in the autumn and winter over at 5–8 °C (41–46 °F). Move it back to a warmer location beginning in February and accustom the plant to the spring sunlight gradually. Buds are very sensitive to frost.

Watering and fertilising Keep the substrate moist at all times during the growing period; do not allow it to dry out. Use only soft water and supplement with a lime-free fertiliser once a week until September. Blue varieties require an additional monthly dose of aluminium sulphate. Water only sparingly in winter.

Care Cut off wilted blossoms to the point of new growth. Older plants may be pruned radically after blooming, if desired. At the end of winter, re-pot hydrangeas in acidic, humus soil – e. g. azalea or rhododendron substrate – and grow back at 15–20 °C (59–68 °F). Low pH is essential for development of blue colour.

Propagation In summer, root top cuttings taken from mature, young shoots at 18–20 °C (64–68 °F) under plastic film. Pinch the tops of the young plants once or twice.

❗ *Caution: Poisonous and/or allergenic*

IMPATIENS

Family Balsams (*Balsaminaceae*)

Origin The vast range of impatiens varieties is the result of intensive selection and hybridisation. The original species comes from New Guinea; many of the approximately 600 species of impatiens are naturally found in the African tropics.

Characteristics This large-blossomed relative of the well known busy Lizzy (*I. walleriana*) is as well suited to indoor cultivation as it is to the garden or patio. It grows in a bushy shape, standing between 20 and 40 cm (8–15 in) tall. Its rounded flowers consist of five petals each and can be found in a wide variety of colours. Houseplants are available on the market throughout the year. Planted outdoors, impatiens will bloom uninterrupted from late spring until autumn. The lancet-shaped leaves, which are finely serrated at the edges, may be green, bronze or yellow and green variegated, depending on the variety.

Location Bright to semi-shady; in sunny locations only with abundant water. Indoor temperatures should be around 18–20°C (64–68°F); place the plant outdoors in the summertime.

Watering and fertilising Keep the substrate well moistened at all times; do not allow it to dry out. At the same time, however, you should not allow standing water to accumulate. Lime-free water is preferable. To encourage blooming, fertilise regularly, once per week from spring until the end of summer.

Care There is no need to re-pot, since the plants are only kept for one season.

Propagation Sow seeds in early spring at around 20 °C (68 °F) and keep them uniformly moist. Top cuttings are easy to root in propagating soil or in a glass of water. The frost-sensitive young plants need to be cultivated indoors until mid-May.

Jasminum officinale
JASMINE

Family Olives (*Oleaceae*)

Origin The true or white jasmine is very widespread. It originated in the Himalayas, Kashmir and south-western China and has been naturalised into Europe. In its natural habitat, it grows as a climbing shrub to lengths of several metres.

Characteristics Potted jasmine plants are usually grown on wire arches and sold at heights of 40–60 cm (15–24 in), but if

cultivated in a container with a trellis, they can grow to much greater heights. Throughout the summer and into autumn, the white, star-shaped flowers with their characteristic fragrance appear above the dark green leaves. The flowers of the 'Grandiflorum' variety may be up to 4 cm (1½ in) in diameter.

Location As bright as possible, but without direct sunlight. In summer the plant enjoys an airy location on a balcony or patio, preferably sheltered by a warm south wall. Winter the plant over at 5–10 °C (41–50 °F).

If jasmine loses its buds, it may be receiving too little water. Loss of leaves in the autumn heralds the winter rest period.

TIP

Watering and fertilising Keep the earth ball slightly moist at all times during the growing period; fertilise once per week. If the plant's location is warm it should be misted frequently. In winter, water just enough that the soil does not dry out.

Care Remove wilted shoots. Depending upon the root development, re-pot the jasmine every one or two years in the springtime, in ordinary potting soil.

Propagation Take non-woody cuttings in the spring or summer. Cultivate them at 20 °C (68 °F) under plastic film and keep them supported.

KALANCHOE

Family Stonecrops (*Crassulaceae)*

Origin This familiar houseplant originally comes from Madagascar, where it grows as a succulent semi-shrub.

Characteristics The dark green, succulent leaves of this approximately 30-cm (12-in) plant grow very close together. From late winter until spring, the inflorescences emerge from the upper leaf axils. Depending upon the variety they may be red, pink, orange, yellow or white. Highly specialised cultivation (darkening) produces plants that bloom throughout the year.

Location As bright as possible, but protected from harsh midday sun. The temperature should be around 20 °C (68 °F) year round; it can be slightly cooler at night. To encourage the plant to bloom again once its flowers have wilted, simulate short days for a period of four to five weeks: the plant should receive nine hours of daylight and be completely darkened the rest of the time (for example, by covering it with a cardboard box).

Watering and fertilising As a succulent, the kalanchoe does not require a great deal of water. Add water only when the surface of the soil is completely dry. If water is allowed to stand, the roots and base of the stem will rot very easily. Fertilise every two weeks from May until August.

Care Remove wilted flowers, cutting back as far as the next leaf. If necessary, you can re-pot the plant in the spring or summer in a sandy substrate or in cactus soil. The new pot should be only slightly larger than the old one.

Propagation Take cuttings during the summer months, after the blooming period; each one should include two or three pairs of leaves. Set them aside for a 24 hours, until a calloused tissue has formed at the cut edge. You can then plant each one in a small pot and cultivate at 20–22 °C (68–72 °F).

191

Lantana Camara hybrids

LANTANA

Family Verbenas (*Verbenaceae*)

Origin This pretty evergreen shrub is native to Mexico and tropical America. The majority of the plants available for purchase are hybrids.

Characteristics Lantana is cultivated both as a bush and as a long-stemmed plant. You have the choice between a small potted plant and large container plants; the latter can grow to heights of 1 m (3 ft) or more. Lantana's elongated green leaves have a corrugated texture. The plant produces clusters of flowers throughout the summer; the flowers are rather unique in that they change their colour over the course of the blooming period. The different varie-

192

ties bloom in shades of red, yellow, pink, cream or white. All parts of the plant are poisonous.

Location Sunny; outdoors beginning in mid-May. The plant should spend the winter in a bright, airy room at temperatures of 5–10 °C (41–50 °F). At winter's end it will need to be re-introduced to brighter sunlight gradually; it should first be placed in a semi-shady location.

Watering and fertilising Water liberally in the summer; larger plants may need to be watered twice a day. Do not allow the substrate to dry out completely, since the leaves will not regenerate quickly once they have turned brown. Fertilise once a week from spring until autumn; water less in the winter.

Care If you remove wilted blossoms frequently, the plant will produce new flowers even more abundantly. In the springtime you can either prune back long shoots or cut the plant back radically. If the lantana's winter quarters are cramped, you can cut it back beforehand and winter it over in the dark at approximately 5 °C (41 °F). Be careful: the irregularly placed stalks have sharp thorns.

Propagation From spring until summer, top cuttings will form roots quickly at 20 °C (68 °F).

! *Caution: Poisonous and/or allergenic*

Lavandula angustifolia

LAVENDER

Family Labiates or mints *(Lamiaceae)*

Origin True lavender is a hallmark of the Mediterranean region, which is also its natural habitat. In addition, fringed or French lavender (*L. dentate*), with its striking spathes at the ends of the flower heads, is being seen more and more frequently.

Characteristics With its compact size of 25–60 cm (10–24 in), this evergreen semi-shrub makes a good pot or container plant for a balcony or patio. Its stems bear needle-shaped, greyish green leaves with an aromatic fragrance, further enhanced in mid-summer by the scent of the flowers clustered in slender spikes. Depending on the variety, they are blue, violet or pink.

Location As sunny and warm as possible. Although this plant will tolerate freezing temperatures as low as −10 °C (14 °F) for short periods, some protection is recommended in winter. To be on the safe side, winter lavender over in a bright, well ventilated room at a maximum temperature of 10 °C (50 °F).

Watering and fertilising

Water regularly in the summer months, keeping the soil slightly moist at all times. Lavender can tolerate overly dry conditions better than overly wet ones. Water very sparingly in the winter. From spring until late summer, fertilise every week, but only in low doses.

Care

In order to maintain bushy growth without bare spots, cut the plant back after the blooming period. Do not cut too far into the older woody sections, however, since the plant cannot easily produce new growth from these areas. Re-pot as necessary in sandy, dry soil.

Propagation

The spring and summer are the best times to take tender or semi-mature cuttings, approximately 10 cm (4 in) long. They will root within four to eight weeks if kept under plastic film at moderate temperatures. A propagating hormone will encourage root development. You can also sow seeds in the early spring.

Lilium hybrids
LILY

Family Lilies *(Liliaceae)*

Origin Mid-century hybrids (Asian lily hybrids) are frequently used as potted plants for the house or patio.

Characteristics Depending on the variety, potted lilies grow 50 to 80 cm (20–31 in) high. The narrow, lancet-shaped leaves are

interspersed along the firm, upright flower stems. In summer – approximately four to five months after planting – several large, usually funnel-shaped flowers appear at the ends of the stems. They may be red, orange, yellow or white.

Location Bright to semi-shady. The flowers will last longest in a cool room (12–16 °C/54–61 °F). Outdoors, the plants should be protected from wind as much as possible. If you have a garden, you can plant the bulbs there after the blooming period; allow the leaves to wilt before doing so.

Watering and fertilising The lily requires a great deal of water when it is in bloom. From the time it is planted until the blooming period, water it only when the surface of the soil is dry. Avoid standing water. The lily does not need large amounts of nutrients. Fertilise every two weeks, but only from the time of germination until flowers develop.

Care Remove wilted flowers regularly. This single-season plant does not need to be re-potted.

Propagation In autumn, place several bulbs in a pot and cover them with soil. The substrate should be humus and rich in nutrients. A layer of potshards or expanded clay at the bottom improves drainage. The bulbs should first be stored at 5–10 °C (41–50 °F) and kept just barely moist. In February and March raise the temperature to 10–12 °C (50–54 °F). As soon as they sprout the plants need light, warmth and more frequent watering.

MAMMILLARIA

Family Cacti (*Cactaceae*)

Origin Most of the plentiful *Mammillaria* species are found in the warm steppes that extend from Mexico to Colombia.

Characteristics Depending on the species and type, these cacti may reach 20 cm (8 in); the shape may be broad and round or tall and cylindrical. They may develop only one head or entire groups of them. The cactus' surface is covered with nipples, each of which bears variously shaped spines. Some species are hairy. Only when the cactus is several years old will yellow, red, violet or white flowers appear around the plant's crown in the spring.

Location As sunny as possible; in fact, the plant needs to receive several hours of direct sunlight each day. During the growing period, daytime temperatures of 25–30 °C (77–86 °F) are ideal; the temperature may drop as low as 16 °C (61 °F) at night. Even in winter, the temperature should be at least 18 °C (64 °F) during the day and 10 °C (50 °F) or more at night.

Watering and fertilising From spring until autumn, water only when the substrate is completely dry; and in winter only when the plant begins to shrivel. It is better to water too little than too much, so that the plant does not rot. Supplement with cactus fertiliser once in the spring.

Care If the cactus's pot becomes too small, you can re-pot it any time, preferably in a sandy cactus substrate.

Propagation Some species produce seeds, which you can sow from spring until autumn, in a sandy soil at a minimum of 20 °C (68 °F). In species that form groups, you can cut off the offshoots, let a callous form on the cut edge, then plant the new cactus in a pot. In some species, offshoots will separate by themselves.

Maranta leuconeura

PRAYER PLANT

Family Prayer plants or arrow roots (*Marantaceae*)

Origin Also called rabbit tracks, it comes from tropical Brazil, where it is a perennial.

Characteristics Prayer plant, which grows to ca. 30 cm (12 in), is beloved for its striking, velvety leaves. They may have widely varying patterns, depending on the type.

Location Semi-shady; protected from direct sun. Prayer plants like warmth and require room and air temperatures of at least 22 °C (72 °F) during the day and 18 °C (64 °F) at night. Humidity should be ca. 60 per cent.

Watering and fertilising The earth ball should always be quite moist; mist daily with soft water. Depending on the temperature in winter, you can water somewhat less. Fertilise at two-week intervals from spring until autumn; the rest of the year, approximately every six weeks.

Care Re-pot in the spring if necessary.

Propagation Separate the root ball carefully in the spring. Continue cultivating the sections under bright, moist conditions at a minimum of 18 °C (64 °F).

Myosotis sylvatica

FORGET-ME-NOT

Family Borages and forget-me-nots (*Boraginaceae*)

Origin The woodland forget-me-not is a native European plant which has spread as far as Asia. Numerous species are now available.

Characteristics The plant forms a rosette of leaves at ground level and grows to 10–30 cm (4–12 in) depending on the variety. It is normally cultivated as an annual or biennial. From early spring until early summer, the blue, pink or white flowers cover the leaves almost completely.

Location Sunny to semi-shady; not too warm.

Watering and fertilising Keep the soil sufficiently moist, but without standing water. A dose of fertiliser before the blooming period will benefit the plant.

Care Cut back any wilted flower stems. The ideal substrate is loose and rich in nutrients.

Propagation You can sow seeds directly in the garden in the summer or indoors in the spring, at temperatures around 18 °C (64 °F). The plant also sows abundant seeds of its own.

Myrtus communis
MYRTLE

Family Myrtles (*Myrtaceae*)

Origin This evergreen shrub can be found in Southern Europe, the Middle East and north-west Africa. It grows up to 3 m (10 ft) high in its natural habitat.

Characteristics Myrtle is available commercially as a potted or container plant. Its natural growth pattern is bushy, but it may also be cultivated as a high-stemmed plant or pyramid. The dark green leaves are lancet-shaped and often grow in groups of three. They emit an intense aroma when rubbed together. From spring until autumn, the myrtle's delicate white blossoms cover the leaves almost entirely.

Location Myrtle likes a sunny, bright and airy location; it is happy in a wind-sheltered spot on a patio in the summer. Indoors, it is content at temperatures between 18 and 20 °C (64–68 °F); temperatures as low as 5 °C (41 °F) are sufficient in winter. It is better to keep the plant too cool than too warm.

Watering and fertilising Water liberally from spring until autumn and mist frequently, but do not allow standing water to accumulate. Add a fertiliser to the water once per week during this period. Reduce watering to a minimum in winter. It is important to use only soft, room temperature water.

Care Younger plants require a fresh substrate every 1–2 years; older specimens may be re-potted every 3–5 years in the spring.

The new pot should not be much bigger than the old one, and the stem should not be covered with soil or it will rot. Do not give the plant a shaping trim every year, since the myrtle will not bloom again that season once it has been pruned.

Propagation In the spring, root semi-mature cuttings without flowers at 18–20 °C (64–68 °F) and pinch the tops several times.

Nephrolepis exaltata

BOSTON FERN

Family Sword ferns *(Nephrolepidaceae)*

Origin These perennial ferns, also known as sword ferns, are at home in the tropical regions of the world, where they some-times grow on trees as epiphytes; however, they produce their own food. Numerous varieties are available commercially.

Boston fern *Nephrolepis exaltata*

Characteristics This bushy, evergreen fern can grow up to 80 cm (31 in) high. Compact varieties, such as 'Teddy Junior' remain much smaller. The feathered fronds are more or less wavy depending on the type, and hang over slightly.

Location Bright to semi-shady, but without direct sunlight; for example, at a north window. Ideally, both air and soil temperatures should be around 18–20 °C (64–68 °F); the plant does not need to be much warmer than this. Be sure that the humidity is at least 50 per cent.

Watering and fertilising Do not allow the earth ball to dry out; keep it slightly moist at all times while still avoiding standing water. It is best to use softened water, with which you should also mist the fern frequently in the summer. If the location is too dry, the fronds will turn brown. Hydroponic culture also works well for this fern. Fertilise once a week from spring until autumn; not at all in the winter.

Care If the Boston fern's pot is too cramped, you can re-pot it in the spring or summer in slightly acidic, loose substrate. For example, you can mix some leaf compost and sand with ordinary potting soil.

Propagation If young plants form from the runners, you can simply separate them and plant them. Spring is the best time for sowing spores. The ideal germinating temperature is 20 °C (68 °F); however, not all varieties will produce spores.

Nerium oleander

OLEANDER

Family Dogbanes (*Apocynaceae*)

Origin An evergreen shrub native to the Mediterranean, north-west Africa and East Asia. Older plants may soar up to 5 m (50 ft).

Characteristics In our latitudes, the warmth-loving oleander is cultivated as a bushy container plant. The shoots are covered with long, narrow, leathery leaves; it blooms in summer. The range of types is great; the flowers, for example, may be pink, red, apricot, yellow or white, simple or compound; and some have a captivating scent. All parts of this plant are poisonous!

Location Oleander only blooms luxuriantly in sunny, warm years. In summer it thrives in a rain-protected spot outdoors. It tolerates negative temperatures for short periods of time, but it is best to winter it over in a bright, cool place in the house (5–8 °C/41–46 °F), for example, a stairwell or winter garden.

Watering and fertilising In the summer, oleander requires large amounts of water and nutrients. It is important to water regularly and liberally; the best approach is to fill the saucer with water. In addition, the plant should be fertilised once per week during the growing period.

Care Wilted flower stems should be left on the plant, since new flowers will develop there in the following year. Older branches that are no longer attractive, however, may be removed in the spring. If necessary, re-pot in the springtime as well.

Propagation To propagate a single species, take cuttings of 10–15 cm (4–6-in) in summer, root them in a glass of water, and then plant in pots. If species purity is not important to you, you can also sow seeds (the ideal temperature for germination is 20–25 °C/68–77 °F). The seeds should be as fresh as possible.

! *Caution: Poisonous and/or allergenic*

Opuntia
PRICKLY PEAR

Family Cacti (*Cactaceae)*

Origin Most species come from the dry regions of South America.

Characteristics The prickly pear's shoots consist of several limbs, which may be disk-shaped, cylindrical or spherical depending on the species. They are often studded with thorns. Flowers also appear in summer.

Location Full sunlight, 20 °C (68 °F) or warmer; no cooler than 8 °C (46 °F) at night. A few species, such as *O. compressa* or *O. engelmannii,* are winter-hardy in our climate, but they require protection from wetness.

Watering and fertilising Water only when the substrate is dry; in winter, only when the plant becomes shrivelled. Cacti will rot easily under wet conditions. Supplement with a flower fertiliser once in the spring and once in summer.

Care Re-pot in cactus substrate every one or two years in the springtime. Scale insects may be a problem.

Propagation Take cuttings in spring; allow the cut edge to dry for 2–3 days and then plant in pots. Sow seeds at approximately 20 °C (68 °F); allow the seeds to pre-germinate in water.

AFRICAN DAISY

Family Daisies and composite flowers (*Asteraceae*)

Origin The parent species of these hybrids originated in South Africa.

Characteristics African daisies are perennials in their natural habitat. As patio plants they grow to ca. 80 cm (31 in) and are usually cultivated as annuals. The dark green leaves are narrow and elongated. The daisy-shaped flowers – white, pink, violet, yellow or crème-coloured, some with eye or spoon-shaped ray florets – appear as early as May. The flowers close in darkness or bad weather.

Location Sunny and warm, protected from wind and rain.

Watering and fertilising Keep the soil slightly moist from spring until autumn; fertilise weekly.

Care African daisies thrive in nutrient-rich, porous substrate. Remove wilted blossoms often. Winter over in frost-free conditions.

Propagation Root cuttings in the spring at temperatures of 18–20 °C (64–68 °F); later, continue cultivating them at about 15 °C (59 °F) and pinch off the tops several times. Sow seeds in December at 22–24 °C (72–75 °F).

Oxalis tetraphylla

SHAMROCK

Family Wood sorrels or sour grasses (*Oxalidaceae*)

Origin This species of wood sorrel, native to Mexico, is often sold under its former name, *O. deppei*. The Andean wood sorrel from Chile, *O. adenophylla*, is frost-hardy and suitable as a balcony or garden plant. It has shiny, silvery leaves and pink flowers with white throats.

Characteristics Botanically, shamrock is a perennial. Its bulb produces the characteristic four clover-like leaves at the end of each long stem; in the well known 'Iron Cross' variety, they are green with reddish-brown centres. The leaves fold together in the evenings. In nature, the delicate pink flowers appear in late summer. The cushion-like plants grow ca. 20 cm (8 in) high.

Location Sunny to semi-shady and not too warm (10–15 °C/ 50–59 °F). Outdoors, the shamrock's location should be protected from the rain.

Watering and fertilising During the growing period, substrate must be moist and must not dry out. Fertilise every two weeks during this time, preferably using softened water.

Care If the pot becomes overly cramped, you can remove the tubers in September, clean them and store them in a dry place at approximately 3 °C (38 °F). Re-plant them in the springtime in a sandy, low-lime substrate.

Propagation Plant bulblets, either purchased or separated while re-potting a plant, in autumn. Place several bulblets in each pot and cover well with soil. Keep the temperature around 8 °C (46 °F) until the plants sprout, then ca. 12–14 °C (54–57 °F); the soil should be slightly moist at all times. You will then be able to give the gift of a "lucky shamrock" for the New Year.

! *Caution: Poisonous and/or allergenic*

Pachypodium lamerei

MADAGASCAR PALM

Family Dogbanes (*Apocynaceae*)

Origin This succulent plant, also known as club foot or elephant's trunk, grows as a tree in its native southern Madagascar.

Characteristics The thick, columnar trunk, which is studded with thorns, is topped by a tuft of long, narrow, dark green leaves. *P. geayi* has more delicate, silver-grey leaves. If its pot is large enough this plant can reach 1 m (3 ft) high. In its natural habitat, the palm produces fragrant white flowers in summer.

Location Sunny and warm. Madagascar palms tolerate temperatures of 30 °C (86 °F) and higher. Unlike cacti, they don't need a cool period in winter and can remain in the living room. The soil temperature in particular should remain above 15 °C (59 °F). Even dry, artificially heated air will not harm the plant.

NOTE *If the leaves turn black or die off, it usually means that the root ball is too wet or too cold.*

Watering and fertilising Keep the substrate just moist; the plant drops its leaves when too dry. Fertilise once a month during the growing period. If the leaves turn yellow in autumn, discontinue watering and fertilising until spring. This succulent plant can store water in its trunk.

Care It is usually sufficient to re-pot the Madagascar palm every two years. Good drainage is very important, so be sure the pot contains drainage holes and place a layer of clay potshards or expanded clay granules on the bottom. Mix potting soil with sand to loosen it, or use a cactus substrate.

Propagation Seed propagation is fairly difficult and is usually done by professionals.

! *Caution: Poisonous and/or allergenic*

213

Paphiopedilum

LADY'S SLIPPER ORCHID

Family Orchids *(Orchidaceae)*

Origin Most of the 60-plus species of lady's slipper orchids are native to South-east Asia and Thailand, and many are protected by conservation laws. Hobby gardeners need not be concerned as most commercially available plants are cultivated hybrids.

Characteristics From late winter until early spring, this orchid's unique flowers emerge from the rosette of long, strap-

shaped leaves. They consist of large, colourful petals and sepals and a distinctive, slipper-shaped lip, which may be yellow, reddish brown or multi-coloured, depending on the variety.

Location Bright to semi-shady. Do not expose the plant to harsh sunlight, particularly in summer. Hybrid varieties usually prefer warm conditions (20–24 °C/68–75 °F or more). In winter the plant appreciates a few hours of morning and evening sun; its location should be no cooler than 18 °C (64 °F), especially at night. It requires a consistent relative humidity of around 60 per cent, but do not mist the flower buds. In summer, lady's slipper orchids can even move to a protected outdoor location.

Watering and fertilising Keep the substrate moderately moist and don't let it dry out; excessive dryness can damage the roots. In winter, when temperatures are lower, the plant should be watered less. Be careful not to water into the heart of the plant. It is best to water in the morning so the orchid has time to dry and will not rot. From spring until autumn, supplement once a month with an ordinary flower fertiliser.

Care Re-pot after blooming, if necessary, in a substrate consisting of one-third peat and two-thirds coarse bark with 2 g/l dolomite limestone. Do not plant the orchid deeper than it was in its previous pot.

Propagation At the time of re-potting, divide the plant carefully so as not to damage the roots.

Passiflora caerulea

PASSION FLOWER

Family Passion flowers (*Passifloraceae*)

Origin This species, a fast-growing climber, is at home in Brazil, Paraguay and Argentina and has been naturalised into the tropics. There are many hybrids available on the market.

Characteristics From summer to autumn, the plant's flowers, up to 9 cm (3.5 in) in diameter, stand out. The petals are usually white to pale pink. The blue and white crosshairs – which are striped in segments – and purple styles are particularly striking. The flowers emerge individually from the leaf axils. The passion flower's leaves have 5 to 7 lobes; they may turn yellow and drop off during the winter rest period. All parts of the plant – except for the ripe fruits – contain poisonous alkaloids.

Location Bright and sunny, but not in harsh sunlight. Passion flowers prefer moderately warm rooms, or a protected spot on the patio in summer. In mild climates it will survive the winter with light protection; safer is to winter it over in a bright spot at 6–12°C (43–54 °F). Keep the humidity around 60 per cent.

Watering and fertilising The passion flower requires a lot of water in summer. Water less in a cool winter location; however, the substrate should still not be allowed to dry out. Fertilise once a week during the growing period, from spring until autumn.

Care Younger potted plants should receive a fresh substrate every year; for older specimens, once every two years is usually sufficient. Around the end of February, prune the plant back radically and re-pot it three to four weeks later. After pruning, keep the passion flower in a shadier location for the first week.

Propagation Take top and shoot cuttings from healthy side branches in the early spring. Allow them to root at around 25 °C (77 °F) under sufficiently moist conditions.

⚠ *Caution: Poisonous and/or allergenic*

Pelargonium grandiflorum

REGAL PELARGONIUM

Family Geraniums and pelargoniums *(Gerania-ceae)*

Origin The original species is native to South Africa and Namibia. The large-flowered varieties are the result of various hybridisations.

Characteristics Botanically speaking, pelargoniums are shrubs. Regal pelargoniums, also known as English geraniums or Martha Washington geraniums, grow between 40 and 80 cm (15–30 in) high, depending on the variety, location and age of the plant. They grow in a bushy shape and are thickly covered with rounded leaves with serrated edges. The fresh green colour of the

leaves contrasts beautifully with the gaily coloured umbels, which appear throughout the summer. They bloom in various shades of pink, red and violet as well as white, sometimes with darker spots.

Location Regal pelargoniums are suitable both as house and patio plants. In the home, they like a bright to sunny and well ventilated location at 18–20 °C (64–68 °F). In the summer, they will do well in a warm, bright to semi-shady spot on the balcony or patio – preferably protected from rain so that the flowers are not damaged. Winter the plants over in a bright and frost-free location; cool temperatures around 10 °C (50 °F) are important for flower development. Nevertheless, after several years the plants will not bloom as abundantly.

Watering and fertilising Keep the earth ball only slightly moist during the summer; in winter, water just enough that the soil does not dry out. To ensure luxuriant blossoming, fertilise the pelargonium every week from spring until early autumn; fertilise every four weeks in winter.

Care Remove wilted flowers regularly. Prune your regal pelargoniums back after the blooming period and before their annual re-potting in the spring.

Propagation Take top cuttings in summer or spring and allow them to root under plastic film at soil and air temperatures of about 20 °C (68 °F). Sow seeds in the springtime.

Pelargonium peltatum, P. zonale

PELARGONIUM, "GERANIUM"

Family Geraniums and pelargoniums *(Geraniaceae)*

Origin This genus, including more than 200 species, originated in South Africa. The plants came to Europe in the 17th century.

Characteristics Horseshoe geraniums (*P. zonale*) grow bushy and upright, to heights of 30–60 cm (12–24 in), while ivy or hanging geraniums (*P. peltatum*) grow long, overhanging or trailing branches. These perennial shrubs are frequently cultivated for just one year, but are well worth wintering over. The blooming period extends from spring to autumn; the umbel-like inflorescences come in a wide range of colours. The flowers may be simple, semi-compound or compound. The leaves are frequently marked with a dark area.

NOTE   *The leaves of scented pelargoniums contain essential oils with fragrances resembling lemon, rose, mint, apple and many other scents.*

Location Sunny, warm, protected from wind and rain. Variegated-leaf varieties will also grow well in semi-shade.

Watering and fertilising Geraniums require a great deal of water in summer. Water regularly and fertilise according to type. Nevertheless, the plants can tolerate dry periods quite well.

Care Compound varieties need to be dead-headed regularly; the simple varieties usually groom themselves. For best results, winter the plants over in a bright location at 10–15 °C (50–59 °F), keeping them relatively dry. If kept in a dark basement over the winter, they will produce new growth very late or not at all. Prune older plants back in spring to encourage better branching.

Propagation The best time to take top cuttings is spring or summer. 20 °C (68 °F) is ideal for root formation. Horseshoe geraniums can be propagated via seeds, but it is a tedious process.

221

Pennisetum alopecuroides

FOUNTAIN GRASS

Family Grasses (*Poaceae*)

Origin This species, which originated in Korea, Japan and the Philippines, is also known as Chinese fountain grass.

Characteristics This grass forms loose copses with its narrow, linear, slightly overhanging leaves. Including its spadix-like inflorescence, fountain grass can grow up to 1 m (3 ft) high, de-

pending on the variety; however, there are also dwarf varieties available for balcony boxes. Its downy-haired ears are reddish-brown; the blooming period is from July to September.

Location This elegant ornamental grass will flourish as a container plant in a sunny, warm location on the balcony or patio. It can be relied on to bloom even in cool summers, and forms an attractive contrast to classic autumn-blooming plants.

Watering and fertilising A nutrient-rich, porous substrate is very important; however, the soil should not be kept overly dry during the growing period. Fountain grass requires only moderate fertilising; it is best to work a time-release fertiliser or an organic fertiliser into the soil. It is imperative to avoid standing water in the wintertime.

Care To keep fountain grass looking attractive, you can remove any wilted leaves in the wintertime. Since the flower stems are highly decorative even in winter, you can wait until spring to prune the plants back. In regions where winters are cold, insulate the container for the winter and cover the plant with a layer of dry mulch.

Propagation You can divide the plant in the spring or early summer. It is a good idea to do this after a few years, when the plant is blooming less abundantly. This vegetative method will produce identical offspring of the same species. You can also sow seeds in spring at temperatures of at least 10 °C (50° F).

PENTAS

Family Coffees and madders *(Rubiaceae)*

Origin This semi-shrub, also known as star cluster or star flower, originally comes from tropical Africa and Arabia.

Characteristics We are familiar with pentas as both a long-stemmed cut flower and a compact potted plant. The latter are treated with growth inhibitors to curb their size and are usually sold at heights of 20–40 cm (8–15 in). The small, star-shaped individual flowers – which may be pink, red, violet or white, depending on the variety – form umbel-like inflorescences which nearly cover the plant's light green leaves. Flowering plants are available almost all year round.

Location Sunny to semi-shady. The room temperature should be around 20 °C (68 °F) and not dip below 10–15 °C (50–59 °F), even in winter. Pentas is also suitable for the patio; however, it is frost-sensitive and should be sheltered from wind and rain outdoors. If the location is too shady, the branches will etiolate.

Watering and fertilising In summer, pentas need a lot of water. Keep the earth ball moist, but not wet, at all times and fertilise weekly. Refrain from fertilising in winter, and water only when the surface of the substrate is dried out. The plant takes a rest period at this time.

Care Re-pot as needed in ordinary potting soil. Pruning back will keep your plant the desired height and encourage branching.

Propagation Take top cuttings in early spring and place them under plastic foil at 22 °C (72 °F) to root. Support and re-pot the young plants several times to encourage bushy growth. Begin fertilising as soon as the first flowers appear. Plants grown from seeds (germination temperature is approximately 20 °C/68 °F) require about five months to begin blooming.

PEPEROMIA

Family Peppers *(Piperaceae)*

Origin The approximately 1,000 perennial species in this genus can be found in the tropical regions of the world.

Characteristics There are numerous species of peperomia. Some, such as *P. caperata* or *P. fraseri,* form rosettes of longer or shorter-stemmed leaves, which often have corrugated surfaces. They remain relatively compact – 10–15 cm (4–6 in) high – and bloom from spring until autumn, producing white or cream-coloured inflorescences. In the case of *P. fraseri*, the flowers also have a lovely scent. *P. obtusifolia* has smooth, fleshy leaves that are distinguished by their yellow-green variegated pattern. This species flourishes well in hydroponic culture.

Location Bright to semi-shady; protected from harsh sunlight. Variegated types show their colours to best advantage in semi-shady conditions. Soil and air temperatures should be at least 15 °C (59 °F); the plant appreciates temperatures of 20 °C (68 °F) and more in summer. Species with softer leaves, such as *P. caperata*, require a relative humidity of at least 50 per cent; thick-leafed species such as *P. obtusifolia* also tolerate dry indoor air.

Watering and fertilising Keep the soil only slightly moist in the summer; do not allow standing water to build up. Mist the plant frequently. Fertilise every two weeks from spring until autumn; once a month in winter. If the earth ball becomes too wet or too cold, the stems and roots will quickly rot.

Care Re-pot every year in the spring or summer.

Propagation Species with woody stems (e. g. *P. obtusifolia*) may be propagated via tender top cuttings placed under plastic film at 18 °C (64 °F). For other species (e. g. *P. caperata*), place leaf cuttings (an entire leaf with a short stem) under plastic foil to root and produce new growth at approximately 20 °C (68 °F). Both methods may be performed in the spring or summer.

Pericallis x hybrida

CINERARIA

Family Daisies and composite flowers *(Asteraceae)*

Origin The species originates in the Canary Islands, where it is a perennial. Almost all commercially available plants are hybrid species. Cineraria is also well known as *Senecio cruentus*.

Characteristics These compact plants are usually 20–30 cm (8–12 in) tall, but miniature forms also exist. The leaves are relatively large, deep green, and triangular or heart-shaped with serrated edges. As early as late winter the large flowers form in thick, clustered umbels above the foliage. The range of colours is dazzling. Do not eat any parts of this plant.

Location Bright, airy and preferably cool: 16–18 °C (61–64 °F) in summer and 10–14 °C (50–57 °F) in winter. Too much warmth makes the plant susceptible to aphids and white flies. 'Senetti' varieties tolerate higher temperatures and bloom for up to eight weeks under these conditions. They also flourish in pre-spring balcony boxes, but will not survive heavy night frosts.

Watering and fertilising Keep the earth ball moist at all times, but avoid standing water. Fertilise weekly in the growing period until flowers appear; otherwise every two weeks.

Care Remove wilted flowers regularly to encourage successive blossoming. Leave some space between individual plants so they have space to develop well. Cineraria is only cultivated for a single season, so re-potting is not required.

Propagation Modern varieties are normally propagated in nurseries. If you are able to acquire seeds, sow them in July to August. Press the fine seeds down lightly and cover with a glass lid with the addition of newspaper to protect them from harsh sunlight. Cultivate at approximately 20 °C (68 °F); keep the soil consistently moist and remove the glass lid after germination.

🛈 *Caution: Poisonous and/or allergenic*

MINIATURE PETUNIA

Family Nightshades (*Solanaceae*)

Origin Million bells, as these distinctive petunias are also called, are the result of hybridisations between various wild South American species. They are also marketed under the name *Calibrachoa* hybrids.

Characteristics This relatively new type of petunia is a compact plant with a bushy, overhanging growth pattern. The flowers are significantly smaller than those of regular petunias; they appear in abundance from spring until autumn. Varieties bearing red, pink, yellow, blue and white flowers are available.

Location Sunny to semi-shady. Since the branches can break easily, place them in a location sheltered from the wind, ideally protected from rain as well.

Watering and fertilising Water liberally throughout the season and fertilise once per week.

Care No special care is necessary.

Propagation The protected species are propagated via cuttings in the springtime; they are normally only cultivated for one year.

HANGING PETUNIA

Family Nightshades *(Solanaceae)*

Origin Surfinia petunias were bred in Japan and have conquered our market in recent years. A large assortment is now available from European growers as well.

Characteristics The branches of these hanging petunias can grow up to 1.5 m (5 ft) long in balcony boxes or hanging baskets. From spring into late autumn, multitudes of large, funnel-shaped flowers appear over the pale green foliage; depending on the variety, they may be violet, red, pink, blue or white. This plant is extremely robust and weather-hardy.

Location Sunny to semi-shady, protected from wind and rain.

Watering and fertilising Surfinas require large quantities of water and nutrients. If not watered sufficiently and fertilised every week, the leaves will turn yellow and the plants will become sickly.

Care Dead-heading is not necessary, which, considering the sticky leaves, is convenient.

Propagation The protected species are propagated in the spring via cuttings and are normally cultivated as annuals.

Phalaenopsis
MOTH ORCHID

Family Orchids (_Orchidaceae_)

Origin The more than 40 species of moth orchids originally come from East Asia and Indonesia, where they are protected by law. Our houseplants are cultivated hybrid varieties.

Characteristics From autumn until midsummer, the striking, butterfly-shaped flowers – to which the moth or butterfly orchid owes its name – appear at the end of its bare flower stem, arranged in panicles or clusters. The light green, fleshy leaves have an elliptical shape.

Location Bright to semi-shady. Sufficient light is particularly important in winter; otherwise the buds fall off. However, the moth orchid won't tolerate direct sunlight; in the wild it grows in the shade of trees. It enjoys warmth in summer (25 °C/77 °F) and winter (20 °C/68 °F). The orchid needs night-time temperatures of about 15 °C (59 °F) for 3–4 weeks in winter to produce new flowers, but the temperature should never fall below this. Keep the relative humidity high, around 70 per cent.

Watering and fertilising Water the moth orchid with soft water when the substrate is dry; it should not be allowed to dry out completely. During the growing period, fertilise with regular flower fertiliser at one-half concentration every two weeks.

Care New flowers and offshoots will form on the wilted flower stems, so they should only be cut back to one-third of their size.

If necessary, re-pot the plant in the spring in special orchid substrate. This is normally needed every two to three years. Do not remove the aerial roots.

Propagation Separate the small offshoots that form on the flower stem and develop roots and re-pot them individually. In nurseries, moth orchids are often propagated via tissue culture.

PHILODENDRON

Family Arum lilies *(Araceae)*

Origin The ca. 350 species are found in the Central and South American tropics. Many are climbing shrubs that grow up trees – thus the Greek name philein "to love", and dendron "tree".

Characteristics Most of our potted plants are in the juvenile stage. The dark green, leathery leaves vary widely in shape, and

234

may change shape as the plant matures. The large, dark green leaves of *P. bipinnatifidum* are deeply lobed. Some varieties of *P. erubescens* have reddish-brown stems and arrow-shaped leaves when the plants are younger ('Red Emerald'); the leaves of others are deeply split in several places ('Emerald King'). *P. scandens* has smaller, heart-shaped leaves and makes a good hanging plant for a shady spot. The plants may also form aerial roots.

Location Most species prefer a bright location away from harsh sunlight; some will also tolerate semi-shade. Temperatures may be as high as 30 °C (86 °F) in the summer, and should not fall below 16 °C (61 °F) in winter. The temperature of the air and soil should be the same. Aim for a relative humidity of 60 per cent; fortunately, however, the plants are not overly sensitive to dry air. Climbing species require supports.

Watering and fertilising In both summer and winter, keep the earth ball slightly moist, but not wet, at all times. If the roots are too cold or too wet they can rot easily. Fertilise weekly from spring until autumn; only about every four weeks in winter.

Care Re-pot as necessary, from spring until autumn.

Propagation Make section cuttings in the summer and allow them to root under plastic film at soil and air temperatures between 25 and 30 °C (77–86 °F). In species that form trunks, you can also propagate via mossing.

ALUMINUM PLANT

Family Nettles (*Urticaceae*)

Origin The numerous *pilea* species can be found in all tropical regions of the world except Australia. In nature, the artillery plant, as it is also called, grows as a perennial.

Characteristics These compact plants generally grow to just 15–20 cm (6–8 in). The leaves are most often egg-shaped with pointed ends and corrugated, partially raised surfaces. In *P. cadierei*, the leaves are dark green and silver striped. *P. crassifolia* 'Moon Valley' has pale green leaves that are brownish-red in the middle. In the *P. involucrata* variety, the dark to brownish-green leaves have silvery stripes. The flowers are not very conspicuous, although they are responsible for the name "artillery plant": they shoot out their pollen in an explosive fashion, creating small floating clouds.

Location Bright to semi-shady, definitely not in direct sunlight. Moderate temperatures between 15 and 20 °C (59–68 °F) are ideal; however, the plant will still flourish at temperatures up to 25 °C (77 °F). In wintertime the location should not be warmer than 10 °C (50 °F).

Watering and fertilising Keep the soil slightly moist at all times. Do not allow standing water to build up, but nor should the substrate be allowed to dry out. Water less in the winter months. It is sufficient to fertilise every two weeks during the vegetation period; every four weeks in winter.

Care Older plants often lose their shape. Cultivating new young plants every year is recommended.

Propagation Restock your collection in spring by taking top cuttings. These may be rooted in a glass of water or in a propagating substrate covered with plastic film at 20 °C (68 °F). To create a bushy plant, place several cuttings together in each pot. Support the young plants if necessary.

237

Plumbago auriculata

LEADWORT

Family Leadworts (*Plumbaginaceae*)

Origin South Africa – thus, it is also known as Cape leadwort.

Characteristics This shrub initially grows upright; later, the branches drape over elegantly. It is also well suited to cultivation as a hlong-stemmed plant. In the summer it is lushly covered with pale blue flowers; the 'Alba' variety has white blossoms. Since the leadwort is frost-sensitive, it is grown as a container plant in our climate.

Location Sunny to semi-shady, warm and protected. Bring the plant indoors before the first frost; it is best wintered over in a bright location (e. g. a stairwell or cool conservatory) at 5–10 °C (41–50 °F). Leadwort can grow quite large and will require plenty of space.

Watering and fertilising Keep the soil consistently moist in summer and fertilise weekly. It will tolerate brief dry periods.

Care Remove wilted flowers regularly. Re-pot in the springtime; thin the branches or cut back radically if necessary.

Propagation Sow seeds in spring at 20 °C (68 °F), or take tender cuttings from early summer. They will rot easily if too moist

Pogonatherum paniceum

MINIATURE BAMBOO

Family Grasses *(Poaceae)*

Origin The miniature bamboo is naturally found in southern China, Malaysia and north-eastern Australia.

Characteristics This elegant plant grows thick and bushy, up to about 40 cm (15 in) high; the delicate stems with narrow, fresh green leaves hang over slightly.

Location Very bright, but without direct sunlight; warm. Even in winter, the location should not be cooler than 18 °C (64 °F). With its overhanging stems, this grass looks very pretty in a hanging basket or on a pedestal; in the summer it can also live outdoors.

Watering and fertilising The substrate should always be well moistened and not allowed to dry out. Mist the plant frequently to maintain high humidity. If the air is too dry the bamboo's leaves will turn brown. Fertilise approximately every two weeks from spring until autumn; do not fertilise in winter.

Care Re-pot every spring in ordinary potting soil.

Propagation Divide the plant when re-potting in the springtime.

239

Primula obconica
GERMAN PRIMROSE

Family Primroses (*Primulaceae*)

Origin This perennial originates in China.

Characteristics The German primrose has rounded, heart-shaped leaves with wavy edges at the ends of long stems. They are crowned by 20–30 cm (8–12 in) flower stalks bearing large umbels. The flowers come in many colours, simple and compound. Due to targeted cultivation, blooming plants are available year round. The plant contains a substance called primin, which can cause allergic skin reactions. Some varieties are bred not to contain primin.

Location Bright, but not harsh sun; cool rooms or sheltered outdoors. 20 °C (68 °F) in summer; 10–15 °C (50–59 °F) in winter.

Watering and fertilising Keep moist, but avoid standing water. Fertilise biweekly from spring until autumn; monthly in winter.

Care Cultivation past the blooming period isn't worth the effort.

Propagation Sow seeds at 20 °C (68 °F) in summer; do not cover (light-germinating). The job is best done by professionals.

! *Caution: Poisonous and/or allergenic*

COMMON PRIMROSE

Family Primroses *(Primulaceae)*

Origin The pure species is native to western and southern Europe. Many large-blossomed varieties are available for purchase.

Characteristics This perennial forms a rosette of spade-shaped, corrugated green leaves. As early as the end of winter, they bring new life to a living room, balcony, patio or entryway with their colourful blossoms and delicate aroma. The plant can tolerate cold, but the flowers do not tolerate frost.

Location Sunny to semi-shady; inside they only last well in a cool room.

Watering and fertilising Keep the substrate well moistened, particularly in a warm room. The primrose's short season makes fertilising unnecessary. However, it is important that the plant grow in a loose, nutrient-rich substrate.

Care Common primroses are usually sold as seasonal products for a single year. However, you can re-plant them in your garden after the blooming period.

Propagation Sow seeds from spring until early summer.

241

Rhododendron simsii

INDIAN AZALEA

Family Heathers (*Ericaceae*)

Origin This species originated in China and Taiwan. It is also known by the names Formosa azalea or Sim's azalea. Most of the plants that grace our windowsills are hybrid varieties.

Characteristics The Indian azalea is an evergreen shrub with elliptical, dark green leaves. From spring until autumn, the foliage is barely visible beneath the plant's myriad blossoms. Red, pink and white usually predominate; depending on the variety, the flowers may also be multi-coloured, simple or compound.

Location Azaleas like a bright and airy location indoors, away from direct sunlight. Once buds begin to form the plant requires temperatures of at least 18 °C (64 °F); it prefers to be cooler in the winter (5–12 °C/41–54 °F). Beginning in May, the azalea can move to a balcony or patio, but the location should be semi-shady. Maintain a relative humidity of at least 50 per cent.

TIP *After purchasing an azalea, accustom it to warm indoor temperatures gradually.*

Watering and fertilising Keep the soil moist at all times from spring until autumn; do not allow it to dry out. This is particularly important during the blooming period, otherwise the buds and flowers may fall off. Water less during the winter; never allow standing water to accumulate. Use only soft water, such as rainwater, even when you regularly mist the leaves.

Fertilise once per week from spring to autumn, every two to three weeks the rest of the year, using special azalea or rhododendron fertiliser.

Care Remove wilted blossoms regularly. Prune the plant back before winter to maintain bushy growth. Re-pot every one to two years as necessary after the blooming period. Use acidic, lime-free azalea substrate.

Propagation Grafting should be done by specialists.

! *Caution: Poisonous and/or allergenic*

Rosa chinensis

MINIATURE ROSE

Family Roses *(Rosaceae)*

Origin As its alternative name implies, the original Chinese rose species comes from China. Numerous compact varieties are available that are ideally suited to indoor cultivation.

Characteristics This bushy little rose plant grows 15–25 cm (6–10 in) high. It delights viewers all summer long with its deli-

cate flowers, which may be red, pink, yellow or white depending on the variety. The leaves are small, green and oval-shaped.

Location Very bright, but away from harsh sunlight. Place the plant in a well ventilated location so that it will not be susceptible to mildew or spider mites. The rose is content at normal room temperature from spring until autumn. In the winter, when it loses its leaves, it prefers a cold place (approx. 5 °C/ 41 °F). Do not move it into the warm living room immediately in the springtime, but let it get accustomed to the warmer temperature gradually. During the summer, the miniature rose is happy to stand in a sunny, protected location outdoors or to be planted in the garden.

Watering and fertilising Always keep the earth ball slightly moist during the growing period; fertilise weekly during this time as well. Keep the plant nearly dry in wintertime.

Care Remove wilted blossoms regularly. You can re-pot the rose in ordinary potting soil every one to two years in spring, before it begins producing new growth. Over the long term, the plant will only develop well if planted in the garden.

Propagation It is worth attempting to take tender top cuttings in the springtime. Treat them with a rooting medium, insert them in moist propagating soil and allow them to root in a shady location under a plastic film cover. Support the young plants to encourage better branching.

AFRICAN VIOLET

Family Gesneriads (*Gesneriaceae*)

Origin East Africa. Of the approximately 20 species, the numerous varieties of S. *ionantha* are the best known.

Characteristics This diminutive evergreen perennial stands little more than 10 cm (4 in) high. Above the dark green, fleshy leaves, cymes of white, pink, red, blue or multi-coloured blossoms appear nearly all year round; they may be simple or compound, smooth or curly.

Location The African violet likes a bright, warm location; however, it will not tolerate blazing sunlight or dry, artificially heated air. If the location is too sunny, brown spots quickly appear on the plant. In order to bloom throughout the year it requires temperatures of at least 18 °C (64 °F), even in winter.

Watering and fertilising Keep the soil consistently moist during the blooming period. However, the plant should never stand in water, or the leaves and flowers will rot easily. Water less in wintertime. It is best to use soft, room temperature water, since African violets prefer a slightly acidic pH value, around 5. Fertilise every one to two weeks from spring until autumn; every four weeks in the winter.

Care Re-pot once per year, in the spring or summer. You can divide the plant at this time, which will also encourage flower production. An ordinary houseplant soil works well as a substrate, or you can use a mixture of humus and peat (or peat substitute) at a 1:1 ratio.

Propagation In the summer, leaf cuttings will root very easily: Stick young, mature leaves in a moist, sandy substrate, cover with foil and keep them at 20–25 °C (68–77 °F). As soon as roots have formed you can re-pot the young plants.

Salvia splendens

SALVIA

Family Labiates, or mints (*Lamiaceae*)

Origin The salvia or scarlet sage originates in Brazil, where it grows as a perennial or semi-shrub. Numerous varieties are available here.

Characteristics Since it is sensitive to frost, salvia is only cultivated as an annual in our climate. The compact potted varieties are usually 20 to 30 cm (8–12 in) tall. From springtime through autumn the plant produces dense clusters of labiate, tube-shaped flowers above its sturdy heart-shaped leaves. The classic varieties have red blossoms; however, pink, violet, salmon and white variations also exist.

Another attractive species is the painted sage
(S. viridis), which has spathes that are actually
more eye-catching than its flowers. These are
arranged in a spiral formation and may be pink,
violet-blue, red or white, depending on the variety.
The perennial common sage or garden sage
(S. officinalis) is also available in decorative
coloured-leaf varieties, which flourish especially
well in balcony boxes.

TIP

Location Sunny and warm, protected from wind and rain.

Watering and fertilising Keep the substrate constantly moist, particularly in the summer. Fertilise weekly during the growing season.

Care To ensure that the plant grows well, plant it in a loose, nutrient-rich substrate. It will continue to bloom uninterrupted if you remove wilted flower axes immediately.

Propagation Sow seeds at 20 °C (68 °F) in early spring and pre-cultivate them indoors. Prop the young plants once to encourage bushy branching. Beginning in mid-May you can replant them outdoors, or sow seeds directly in the garden. If you do, however, the plants will bloom significantly later.

Schefflera arboricola
DWARF UMBRELLA TREE

Family Aralias *(Araliaceae)*

Origin The dwarf umbrella plant, or dwarf schefflera, originally comes from Taiwan. There it grows as a tree.

Characteristics Umbrella trees a favourite decorative foliage plant. Their striking long-stemmed leaves are divided like umbrella spokes or the fingers of a hand. Individual leaves, which may be solid green or variegated yellow depending on the variety, have rounded edges. *S. actinophylla* is a larger species and has multi-sectioned leaves, up to 30 cm (12 in) in diameter, with pointed ends. All the species quickly grow into bushy plants. Typical of the false aralia (*S. elegantissima*) is its filigreed, multi-sectioned leaves. It requires warm conditions year round.

Location Bright to semi-shady, protected from direct midday sun. Indoor temperatures of 18–20 °C (64–68 °F) or more are best; somewhat cooler in the winter, but not below 12 °C (54 °F). If it is too cold, the umbrella tree will respond by losing its leaves. During the summer it can stand in a semi-shady, wind-protected location outdoors. Mist the leaves frequently to maintain a relative humidity as close to 60 per cent as possible.

Watering and fertilising Keep the earth ball fairly moist, but avoid standing water. Water and mist with room temperature water. Dwarf umbrella trees are very well suited to hydroponic culture. They require a weekly dose of fertiliser from spring through autumn; once a month is sufficient in winter.

Dwarf umbrella tree *Schefflera arboricola*

Care Depending on the size of the pot, re-pot every one to three years in the spring in fresh, nutrient-rich potting soil.

Propagation You can sow seeds any time of year, or attempt to propagate via cuttings. Air and soil temperatures around 22 °C (72 °F) are necessary in both cases; propagation is not easy.

Schlumbergera hybrids

CHRISTMAS CACTUS

Family Cacti (_Cactaceae_)

Origin Various species of this jointed cactus live in the mountainous forests of Brazil. Our houseplants are hybridisations.

Characteristics The plant's overhanging branches consist of several flat, sharply serrated joints. From approximately Christmastime until late winter, the cactus produces large pink, red, violet or white blossoms at the ends of its branches – a trait that

gave the plant its name. To ensure abumdant blossoming, keep the plant in a cool place (8–10 °C/46–50 °F) for approximately six weeks beginning in mid-September; it should receive only eight to nine hours of daylight during this period.

Location Bright to semi-shady, no harsh sunlight. This cactus does best at a south-east or west window and can even live outdoors in summer. It prefers indoor temperatures of 18–20 °C (64–68 °F) all year (as low as 10 °C/50 °F at night). Once flower buds have formed, do not move the plant or the buds will fall off.

Watering and fertilising Keep the soil slightly moist during the budding and blooming periods and fertilise once per month (preferably with a flowering plant fertiliser). Observe a rest period after the blooming phase: For the next eight weeks, water only when the plant begins to shrivel, and withhold fertiliser completely. It is best to use room temperature water.

Care The Christmas cactus only needs re-potting every three to four years. It is best to use a special cactus substrate with a pH value between 4.5 and 5.5. Scale insects can be a problem.

Propagation Take branch cuttings from spring until summer (except during the budding period). Cut off young limbs with two or three segments, allow the cut edge to dry and place in cactus substrate. Keep the cuttings in a bright place, out of direct sunlight, and only mist occasionally. They root quickly at around 22 °C (72 °F); in a year you will have new, blooming plants.

Scindapsus pictus

SATIN POTHOS

Family Arum lilies *(Araceae)*

Origin This evergreen climbing plant originates in Malaysia. It should not be confused with the speckled pothos (*Epipremnum pinnatum*).

Characteristics The satin pothos's most eye-catching feature is its heart-shaped, leathery leaves, which are green with a striking silvery-white speckled pattern. The leaves change their shape as they grow older. They not only become much larger, they are become more elliptical in shape and deeply grooved. The branches of the satin pothos can grow several metres long and may hang down from a shelf or be secured to a trellis.

Location Bright to semi-shady, out of reach of harsh sunlight. Temperatures should be between 18 and 20 °C (64–68 °F) all through the year, with a relative humidity of approximately 60 per cent. Scindapsus enjoys living in close contact with other plants. If you have an enclosed plant window, a satin pothos is a perfect choice.

Watering and fertilising The substrate should always be kept slightly moist and not allowed to dry out. It is best to use room temperature water. Hydroponic culture makes the plant's water requirements even easier to maintain. In order to ensure high humidity, mist the leaves regularly with soft, room-temperature water. Add a fertiliser to the plant's water every 1–2 weeks from spring until autumn; in winter, every 3–4 weeks.

Care Re-pot the satin pothos in fresh soil in the spring. For older specimens in large pots, re-potting every two years is sufficient.

Propagation Take top or branch cuttings at any time of year. They should contain at least two leaves and be cultivated under plastic film at a temperature of 25 °C (77 °F). Begin supporting the young plants as soon as they have formed enough roots, so that they will develop bushy branches.

❗ *Caution: Poisonous and/or allergenic*

Sedum morganianum

SEDUM

Family Stonecrops (*Crassulaceae*)

Origin This species, which originates in Mexico, is also known as donkey's tail.

Characteristics With its trailing branches, which grow up to 50 cm (20 in) long, this *Sedum* species is an excellently choice for hanging baskets. The branches are covered on all sides with

fleshy, bluish-frosted leaves about 1 cm (½ in) long. Another pretty hanging plant is S. *sieboldii*, which has rounded blue-green leaves with red edges.

Location Sunny, warm and well ventilated. The sedum requires daytime temperatures of at least 20 °C (68 °F) in the summer; it may be somewhat cooler at night. It is even possible to place it in a dry area of the balcony during the warm season. In the wintertime the plant prefers to be cooler, at a maximum temperature of 18 °C (64 °F).

Watering and fertilising Keep the soil moderately moist in summer; it is best to water only when the substrate has dried out. Reduce watering to a minimum in winter. Fertilise every month from March through August with cactus fertiliser.

Care Re-pot the sedum every one or two years, as necessary. Mix regular potting soil with one-third sand, or simply use cactus substrate. Take care to handle the plant gently, as the individual leaves fall off immediately with rough treatment. Refrain from fertilising for six months after re-potting.

Propagation Cut off single leaves or the tips of branches in spring or summer. Let them to dry for several days until a callous tissue develops. Stick the cuttings in gravely cactus substrate, place in a warm, well ventilated location and keep the soil just moist. Leaf cuttings will also form roots on moist newspaper in a semi-shady location at around 15 °C (59 °F).

Solanum jasminoides

POTATO VINE

Family Nightshades (*Solanaceae*)

Origin This evergreen climbing plant comes from the tropics of Brazil, where it can grow to heights of several metres. It has become a common sight in the Mediterranean region.

Characteristics Since it is frost-sensitive, potato vine is a container plant in our climate. Its long, thin branches will cover a trellis or arbour with green in no time, or place it next to a tree and let it climb right up the trunk. Most young leaves have three to five sections; older ones are lancet-shaped and up to 8 cm (3 in) long. The clusters of white (or occasionally light blue) flowers are a striking contrast to the green foliage. In a conservatory potato vine will bloom nearly year round; outdoors it blooms from spring until well into autumn. All parts of the plant are poisonous.

Location Sunny to semi-shady. Flowers are most abundant in warmer years. Although potato vine tolerates temperatures just below freezing, it is best wintered over at about 5 °C (41 °F) in a spot with good ventilation. Kept in the dark in winter it loses all its leaves and produces new growth late in the new season.

Watering and fertilising Water liberally from spring through the summer; fertilise weekly. On hot days, larger plants may need water twice. If water or nutrients are lacking, the lower leaves vine will turn yellow, then fall off. In winter, water just enough that the root ball does not dry out.

Potato vine *Solanum jasminoides*

Care If needed, prune back before moving to its winter quarters; spring pruning is preferable. Re-pot in standard soil as needed.

Propagation You can cultivate cuttings any time from spring until autumn at 20–25 °C (68–72 °F). To encourage full growth, prop the new plants several times.

! *Caution: Poisonous and/or allergenic*

Solanum rantonnetii

BLUE POTATO BUSH

Family Nightshades (_Solanaceae_)

Origin The blue potato bush, alternatively called Paraguay nightshade, comes from Argentina and Paraguay. It has recently been classified botanically as _Lycianthes rantonnetii_.

Characteristics This container plant can be a bushy shrub or a long-stemmed plant. Its delicate branches bow over elegantly, bearing lancet-shaped leaves up to 10 cm (4 in) long. In a bright conservatory, the violet-blue flowers with yellow centres appear nearly year round; otherwise the plant blooms from spring until autumn. The flowers are followed by red fruits ca. 2 cm (¾ in) in diameter. All parts of this nightshade are poisonous.

Location Very sunny and warm.

Watering and fertilising See S. _jasminoides_.

Care Wintered in a bright location at about 10 °C (50 °F), it will retain its leaves and produce new growth quickly in the spring; a dark winter slows the plant's development. Prune in spring, if possible.

Propagation See S. _jasminoides_.

! _Caution: Poisonous and/or allergenic_

MIND-YOUR-OWN-BUSINESS

Family Nettles (*Urticaceae*)

Origin The Balearic Islands, Corsica and Sardinia. This perennial has been naturalised into Southern and Western Europe.

Characteristics Low-growing, ground-covering plants with very small, rounded, fresh green leaves; in some varieties, they may be silvery white or golden yellow.

Location Bright to semi-shady, protected from intense midday sun. Room temperature or cooler (as low as 5 °C/41 °F in winter). Take outdoors in summer; this plant is even winter-hardy in mild areas.

Watering and fertilising Keep the soil consistently slightly moist; do not allow it to dry out even in the winter. From spring until autumn it is sufficient to add a fertiliser to the water every two weeks; fertilise every four to six weeks in winter.

Care Prop the plant regularly to help maintain its compact shape. Rejuvenate it by dividing in the spring and re-planting in fresh potting soil.

Propagation Divide in the springtime, or separate any offshoots that have formed roots.

261

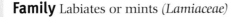

COLEUS

Solenostemon scutellarioides

Family Labiates or mints (*Lamiaceae*)

Origin These colourful plants originate in tropical Africa. There are countless varieties, which are still frequently marketed under their former name, *Coleus Blumei* hybrids.

Characteristics Fast-growing, decorative foliage plants that grow reach 20 to 50 cm (8–20 in), depending on the variety. The

leaves are a multitude of shapes and colours; most are patterned in several shades of green, red, brown or yellow. They may be oval, heart-shaped or elongated, with smooth, serrated or wavy edges. The small, bluish-white flowers are fairly inconspicuous.

Location Sunny to shady; however, the leaves' colours are most intense in a bright location. The plants should be protected from hot midday sun. In the summer coleus prefers temperatures of 20–25 °C (68–77 °F); it is suitable for a patio or garden. In winter it likes to be somewhat cooler (around 18 °C/64 °F).

Watering and fertilising Keep the substrate constantly moist, particularly in warm, bright locations. Water less in the wintertime. Do not allow standing water to accumulate, and use only softened water. Fertilise weekly from spring until autumn.

Care If you pinch off the flowers, the upper leaves will grow larger. Coleus is most attractive when cultivated new each year, but it can be re-potted in slightly acidic soil (mix potting soil with a little peat) and cut back radically. Plants that are not propped will eventually become bare-looking.

Propagation Cuttings can be taken from spring until the end of summer. They will develop roots quickly in a glass of water and may then be planted in pots. Alternatively, place them directly in propagating soil under a plastic cover. Keep the temperature around 20 °C (68 °F) and prop the young plants several times. You can also sow seeds in spring at 20 °C (68 °F).

Sparrmannia africana

AFRICAN HEMP

Family Lindens *(Tiliaceae)*

Origin This evergreen shrub – also called African linden or Cape stock-rose – is a native of South Africa. There, it can grow to heights of up to 6 m (20 ft).

Characteristics In a pot or container this bushy plant stays much smaller than in its natural habitat. At 2 m (7 ft) you will have a stately specimen. The African hemp's leaves are heart-shaped, pale green and up to 15 cm (6 in) long. The plant's most attractive feature is its white blossoms, which appear in large umbels and bear golden yellow stamens. The main blooming period is from January to April.

Location Bright, sunny and well ventilated. The plant does not appreciate harsh midday sun, nor too much shade. It prefers a cool room (15–18 °C/59–64 °F), but will also flourish at normal room temperature. It requires a cool location during the winter months (approximately 10 °C/50 °F) in order to produce flowers. In summer it can live as a container plant in a sheltered spot on a balcony or patio. African hemp is extremely sensitive to frost.

Watering and fertilising The African hemp requires large amounts of water during the growing period. The earth ball should be kept moist at all times, but do not allow standing water to build up. Water less in the winter when the plant's location is cooler. Fertilise weekly from spring until autumn; every three to four weeks for the rest of the year.

Care Cut back the branches by half in spring. If the plant has lost a lot of leaves during winter you can cut it back still further. Re-pot every 2–3 years in standard potting soil or container plant soil, after the blooming period. Always prune after re-potting.

Propagation Take top cuttings from the side branches of the flower stems; root them under plastic film at ca. 20 °C (68 °F).

Spathiphyllum wallisii

PEACE LILY

Family Arum lilies (*Araceae*)

Origin This species originates from Colombia and Venezuela.

Characteristics The peace lily produces a thick cluster of large, long-stemmed leaves that may be up to 20 cm (8 in) long. The leaves have a narrow lancet shape and are a glossy, dark green colour. The main blooming period extends from March to September, when the creamy white, fragrant flower spadices are

surrounded by greenish-white spathes, which tower above the plant's leaves. At 60–80 cm (24–31 in) high, hybrid varieties are larger than the pure species. All parts of the peace lily are poisonous; its sap can cause skin irritations.

Location Semi-shady to shady from spring until autumn; as bright as possible in winter, but always protected from direct sunlight. This tropical species likes warm, moist conditions. If possible, the temperature should not fall below 18 °C (64 °F); it can be quite a bit warmer in the summer. Keep the relative humidity high. A bathroom is an ideal location for a peace lily.

Watering and fertilising Always keep the soil slightly moist and do not allow it to dry out, even in winter. During the growing period, from spring until autumn, fertilise once per week and mist the plant frequently. Fertilise every two to three weeks in winter. The peace lily grows well in hydroponic culture.

Care Depending on the size of the pot, re-plant every one to two years in good-quality potting soil.

Propagation The peace lily develops rhizomes, which you may separate in the springtime in larger plants. Proceed carefully, taking care not to damage the roots. To create a bushy plant from the beginning, place several sections together in one pot and continue cultivating them at approximately 20 °C (68 °F).

! *Caution: Poisonous and/or allergenic*

Tagetes patula
MARIGOLD

Family Daisies and composite flowers (*Asteraceae*)

Origin Mexico and Guatemala

Characteristics Most varieties of this annual summer flower are about 20 cm (8 in) high, some a bit larger. The stems, which are covered with delicate, feathery leaves, are topped by the simple or compound flowerheads throughout the summer. They may be yellow, orange, red, brown or bicoloured. The flowers are significantly smaller than those of the giant marigold (*T. erecta*), but they are more numerous and less sensitive to rain. The leaves and sap of marigolds may cause allergic reactions.

Location Sunny to semi-shady. Appropriate for plant containers and garden beds.

Watering and fertilising Keep the substrate slightly moist from spring until autumn and fertilise once per week.

Care Remove any wilted flowers regularly. Plant the flowers in loose, nutrient-rich soil.

Propagation Sow seeds late winter/early spring at 18 °C (64 °F).

! *Caution: Poisonous and/or allergenic*

Thunbergia alata

BLACK-EYED SUSAN

Family Acanthus or black-eyed Susans *(Acanthaceae)*

Origin This species originates in tropical Africa.

Characteristics In our latitudes, this frost-sensitive climbing plant is cultivated as an annual. Within one year, it can grow up to 2 m (7 ft) high on a trellis. The hairy leaves have a broad arrow shape. Throughout the summer, they are covered with round flowers, which may be yellow, shades of orange or white, depending on the variety. Most have dark-coloured centres.

Location Sunny and warm, protected from wind and rain.

Watering and fertilising Keep the earth ball uniformly moist. However, the plant will tolerate short periods of dryness better than standing water.

Care Plant the black-eyed Susan in loose, nutrient-rich soil.

Propagation Sow seeds in early spring at about 19–20 °C (66–68 °F). Plant several seedlings together in a pot and secure them to posts early on.

269

Tillandsia cyanea
TILLANDSIA

Family Pineapples *(Bromeliaceae)*

Origin Most of the nearly 400 species of *Tillandsia* are native to South America, where these "air plants" grow in cracks of rocks or as epiphytes on trees. This species originates in Ecuador.

Characteristics *T. cyanea* has leaves up to 30 cm (12 in) long which form a rosette. The arrow-shaped inflorescence emerges from its centre. It consists of bright pink spathes; the actual blue-violet flowers perch between them. In addition to the green-leafed species there are also grey-leafed tillandsias, which absorb water and nutrients through their scaly leaves. They need to be misted regularly – from spring through autumn – with a special fertiliser solution (or hydroponic fertiliser).

Location Bright, but not in harsh sunlight. The temperature should be at least 20 °C (68 °F) all year round, with a relative humidity of approximately 60 per cent.

Watering and fertilising Always keep the substrate slightly moist; neither too wet, nor should it dry out. Use soft, room temperature water at all times; pour some water into the leaf cistern as well. Mist the plant frequently. Supplement with a flower fertiliser at one-half concentration once per month.

Care Re-pot the tillandsia every one to three years, as necessary. The soil should have a low pH value (approx. 5) and be humus and coarsely structured; a special bromeliad soil is ideal.

Propagation Older plants frequently produce offshoots, which you can separate and plant in a sandy propagating substrate. The best time to do this is in the spring. Continue cultivating the new plants at approximately 21 °C (70 °F) with high humidity.

Tolmiea menziesii

PIGGYBACK PLANT

Family Saxifrages (*Saxifragaceae*)

Origin This genus consists of only one species, which is found in Alaska, Canada and the north-western United States. There, this runner-forming perennial frequently grows as a ground cover.

Characteristics The bushy piggyback plant grows 20–30 cm (8–12 in) high. Its shield-shaped leaves have notched edges and

are sinuated at the stem joint. Tiny brood buds form exactly at this point and develop into plantlets, giving the plant its many descriptive names: piggyback plant, youth-on-age or mother of thousands. The greenish-brown flowers appear in early summer. In addition to the solid colour species, there are also variegated types with creamy-white patterned leaves. The piggyback plant is an excellent choice for a hanging basket.

Location Semi-shady to shady. If the location is too sunny, the leaves will turn brown quickly. The piggyback plant prefers cool temperatures and can spend its summers outdoors. In winter the temperature should be 10 °C (50 °F) or cooler. In milder climates, this perennial can survive if planted in the garden.

Watering and fertilising Keep the earth ball only moderately moist. Particularly in the winter, when the location is cool, water the plant very sparingly. Fertilise weekly from spring until autumn; every four to six weeks in winter.

Care Re-pot every year in the spring or summer, in fresh, porous potting soil.

Propagation The plantlets will root best if you stick them in a pot containing moist propagating soil, keep them warm, and separate them from the parent plant only after they take root. You can also lay them directly on top of a moist substrate and press them down firmly. In addition, it is possible to divide the plant in the spring.

Torenia fournieri

WISHBONE FLOWER

Family Figworts *(Scrophulariaceae)*

Origin Tropical regions of South Vietnam

Characteristics Depending on the variety, these annuals grow 15–20 cm (6–8 in) high. The blue-flowering variety 'Summer Wave' forms long, overhanging branches. The unusual, throat-shaped flowers appear from summer until autumn. They are usually bicoloured, in shades of blue, violet, pink and red, with contrasting spots on the edges and yellow-spotted centres.

Location Bright to semi-shady or even shady; avoid the blazing midday sun. Indoor temperatures should be at least 18 °C (64 °F) throughout the year, with a relative humidity around 50 per cent. Outdoors, choose a protected spot for this plant.

Watering and fertilising Water regularly, but do not allow standing water. Fertilise once per week from spring until autumn.

Care Cultivate new plants every year.

Propagation Sow seeds at 20–22 °C (68–72 °F) in early spring. Cover the propagating container with plastic film or glass. Later, continue cultivating the young plants at 10–15 °C (50–59 °F).

SPIDERWORT

Family Spiderworts (*Commelinaceae*)

Origin The approximately 70 species of evergreen perennials have their native homes in tropical South America.

Characteristics The spiderwort's branches grow hanging over or lying on the ground, making it an ideal candidate for a hanging basket. Its elongated, pointed and often strikingly patterned leaves are its most dramatic feature. Depending on the species and type, they may be silvery, white or yellow striped, tri-coloured, or brownish on the surface with red undersides. The white flowers that appear in spring are barely noticeable.

Location Bright, or even semi-shady in the summer; avoid midday sun. Keep at 18–20 °C (64–68 °F) in the growth period; temperatures can go as low as 10°C (50°F) in winter.

Watering and fertilising Keep the soil moist in spring through autumn and fertilise every two weeks; mist the leaves frequently. In winter, water less and fertilise monthly.

Care Re-pot in the spring.

Propagation Take top cuttings in the spring and allow them to root in a substrate or a glass of water at room temperature.

Verbena hybrids
VERBENA

Family Verbenas _(Verbenaceae)_

Origin The ancestors of our garden verbenas come from South America, where they grow as perennials or shrubs.

Characteristics In our climate frost-sensitive verbenas are annuals. Depending on the variety they grow in a compact, bushy shape, 20–40 cm (8–15 in) high, or with overhanging branches. Their colourful flowers are usually accented by a white eye. In addition, there are abundantly blooming hanging verbenas whose branches can grow several metres long. The flowers appear throughout the summer in a wide variety of colours.

Location Sunny and warm, protected from rain and wind (especially hanging verbenas).

Watering and fertilising The substrate should not dry out, nor should it be constantly wet. Particularly during the blooming period, fertilise weekly.

Care Remove wilted flowers regularly. Plant verbenas in nutrient-rich, sandy soil.

Propagation Sow seeds in spring at 18–20 °C (64–68 °F). Hanging verbenas are propagated professionally via cuttings.

VIOLA

Family Violets *(Violaceae)*

Origin This little perennial is prevalent throughout central Europe. Breeding has produced myriad hybrids.

Characteristics At 10–15 cm (4–6 in), the horned violet or Johnny jump-up – as viola is also known – is relatively compact. Some varieties grow in an overhanging pattern and are beautiful in hanging baskets. The delicate flowers add colour to balconies or patios from spring until autumn. Depending on the variety, they may be solid or multi-coloured, often with a contrasting eye and fine, dark lines. Leaves are deep green, elongated and have notched edges.

Location Semi-shady, also sunny, preferably cool. In a warm room the branches will become long and thin.

Watering and fertilising Keep the soil sufficiently moist; the plant will tolerate dry periods better than constant wetness.

Care Plant in loose, very humus soil.

Propagation Viola may be cultivated as an annual or as a biennial: Sow seeds in December-January or in June-July. Germinate at 15–20 °C (59–68 °F); continue cultivating at ca. 10 °C (50 °F).

Vriesea splendens

FLAMING SWORD

Family Pineapples *(Bromeliaceae)*

Origin This species is native to the rainforests of Venezuela and Guyana. Various hybrids are available commercially.

Characteristics This perennial plant forms a thick rosette of long, narrow, sturdy leaves. Depending on the variety, they may be decorated with olive green or reddish-brown horizontal stripes. The long (up to 70 cm/28 in) flower stalk emerges from the centre of the rosette. It consists of a sword-shaped flower head made up of gleaming red spathes, between which the yellow flowers appear. The blooming period depends upon artificial cultivation in the nursery.

Location Bright and warm throughout the year, but do not place the flaming sword in direct summer sunlight. A south-east or west-facing window is ideal. The air and soil temperatures should be at least 20 °C (68 °F); avoid radical changes in temperature. Keep the relative humidity at about 60 per cent.

Watering and fertilising Water regularly with soft, room temperature water, adding a little water to the leaf funnel. The substrate should be moist at all times; however the plant will tolerate neither standing water nor over-dryness. Mist the bromeliad frequently, particularly on hot days. Fertilise every two weeks at one-half concentration from spring to autumn; every four weeks is sufficient in winter.

Care If the pot becomes too crowded, re-pot in the spring in loose, part-peat potting soil or bromeliad substrate. It is not necessary to re-pot every year. With the necessary humidity, the flaming sword is a long-lived and low-maintenance plant.

Propagation When offshoots are about 15–20 cm (6–8 in) tall, you can separate them in the spring or summer, re-plant them and allow them to root at ca. 25 °C (77 °F) with high humidity.

Yucca elephantipes

SPINELESS YUCCA

Family Agaves (*Agavaceae*)

Origin The evergreen yucca has its native home in Mexico and Guatemala, where it grows as a tree, to heights of several metres. From summer until autumn, older plants produce white flowers which sit together in large clusters.

Characteristics This succulent plant forms rosettes of narrow, sturdy, upright leaves from shoots that emerge at the end of its scaly trunk. Depending on species and variety, they are green or blue-green. The yucca grows up to 2 m (7 ft) high in a container.

Location Bright all year round; a sunny, protected spot outdoors is ideal in summer. Indoors, the yucca likes well ventilated rooms. It prefers cooler air in winter (5–10 °C/41–50 °F).

Watering and fertilising Water regularly during the vegetation period. In the winter, when the plant's location is cooler, water just enough that the root ball does not dry out. If water is allowed to stand, the roots can rot. On the other hand, the tips of the leaves will turn brown if the plant is too dry. Fertilise every two weeks from spring until late summer; otherwise not at all. In dry, indoor conditions, mist the leaves frequently. Yuccas grow very well in hydroponic culture.

Care Re-pot as necessary in spring in sandy potting soil, including a drainage layer of clay potshards or expanded clay at the bottom of the pot. If the plant grows too large, you can saw it off and it will produce new growth. Coat the cut edge with tree wax.

Propagation Older plants form runners at the base of the trunk, which you can separate when they are about 20 cm (8 in) high. After re-potting, place the young plants in a warm location (20–25 °C) and keep them well moistened. You can also cut off trunk sections and cultivate them in the same manner.

Zamioculcas zamiifolia

AROID PALM

Family Arum lilies (*Araceae)*

Origin This succulent perennial originally is from East Africa. It is a relative newcomer to the houseplant assortment.

Characteristics Strong, fleshy stalks develop from the tuber; they are thickened at the bottom and capable of storing water. The small, oval-shaped leaves are hard and, like the fronds, are a shiny dark green. The plant contains poisonous substances.

Location The aroid palm grows rapidly in a bright location. In a shady spot the leaves turn deep green. Warm, ca. 20 °C (68 °F).

Watering and fertilising Keep the substrate consistently moist, but do not over-water or the leaves will quickly turn yellow. The plant will tolerate dry conditions better than standing water. Mist the leaves occasionally and fertilise at low doses during the growing period; the plant will then produce new fronds regularly.

Care Re-pot in spring, if necessary, in nutrient-rich potting soil. Tolerates being turned toward the light.

Propagation Remove one leaf and stick the injured edge in propagating substrate; cover with glass or plastic film and keep the soil uniformly moist.

! *Caution: Poisonous and/or allergenic*

Zantedeschia aethiopica

CALLA LILY

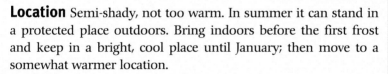

Family Arum lilies *(Araceae)*

Origin South Africa, where it grows in marshlands that are dry in the summer.

Characteristics The fleshy flower stalk can be up to 80 cm (31 in) high. Yellow spadices appear from winter to spring, surrounded by spathes of white or other colours. In the rest period – late May until July – the plant loses its large, arrow-shaped, deep green leaves. All parts are poisonous.

Location Semi-shady, not too warm. In summer it can stand in a protected place outdoors. Bring indoors before the first frost and keep in a bright, cool place until January; then move to a somewhat warmer location.

Watering and fertilising Water liberally during the growing period and fertilise biweekly. Keep the plant drier during the rest period, but do not allow the rhizome to dry out.

Care Re-pot the rhizome in fresh, nutrient-rich flower soil at the end of the rest period.

Propagation Divide rhizome when re-potting, or separate offshoots. Cultivate at ca. 15 °C (59 °F).

! *Caution: Poisonous and/or allergenic*

INDEX